IMAGES OF WAR

M29 Weasel Tracked Cargo Carrier & Variants

IMAGES OF WAR

M29 Weasel Tracked Cargo Carrier & Variants

RARE PHOTOGRAPHS FROM WARTIME ARCHIVES

DAVID DOYLE

Pen & Sword
MILITARY

AN IMPRINT OF PEN & SWORD BOOKS TD.
YORKSHIRE - PHILADELPHIA

First published in Great Britain in 2019 by
Pen & Sword Military
An imprint of
Pen & Sword Books Ltd
Yorkshire – Philadelphia

ISBN 978 1 52674 356 5

Typeset in 12/14.5 Gill Sans by
Aura Technology and Software Services, India

Printed and bound in China by Printworks Global Ltd

Pen & Sword Books Limited incorporates the imprints of Atlas, Archaeology, Aviation, Discovery, Family History, Fiction, History, Maritime, Military, Military Classics, Politics, Select, Transport, True Crime, Air World, Frontline Publishing, Leo Cooper, Remember When, Seaforth Publishing, The Praetorian Press, Wharncliffe Local History, Wharncliffe Transport, Wharncliffe True Crime and White Owl.

For a complete list of Pen & Sword titles please contact

PEN & SWORD BOOKS LIMITED
47 Church Street, Barnsley, South Yorkshire, S70 2AS, England
E-mail: enquiries@pen-and-sword.co.uk
Website: www.pen-and-sword.co.uk

Or
PEN AND SWORD BOOKS
1950 Lawrence Rd, Havertown, PA 19083, USA
E-mail: Uspen-and-sword@casematepublishers.com
Website: www.penandswordbooks.com

Contents

Acknowledgments

This book would not have been possible without the generous help of David Welch, one of the foremost Weasel restoration experts in the country, as well as my friends Tom Kailbourn, Jim Gilmore, John Adams-Graf, Chris Hughes, Rick Forys, Scott Taylor, Rick Wark, Rob Walsh and the late Kevin Kronlund. Thanks also go to the staff and volunteers at the Studebaker National Museum Archives. As always, my wife Denise made significant contributions by scanning vintage photos and hundreds of pages of original documents, and most of all by her unflagging support. All photos, unless otherwise noted, were taken by the author.

Introduction

The Weasel owes its existence – but not its design – to an eccentric Englishman, Geoffrey Pike. Pike, a journalist who later fancied himself an inventor, proposed several unorthodox weapons and campaigns during the Second World War, and he found favor with Chief of Combined Operations Admiral Louis Mountbatten.

Pike convinced Mountbatten that Norway should be infiltrated by small teams of commandos using specialized snow vehicles to execute sabotage tactics that would deprive Germany of hydroelectric power. A joint US–Commonwealth mission was proposed to carry this out, and soon enough US Army Chief of Staff George C. Marshall was briefed on the plan and decided the US industry could produce a suitable vehicle.

The proposed assault was codenamed Operation Plough, and was to have been carried out by the First Special Service Force, a specially-formed elite joint US and Canadian unit.

The development of the special snow vehicle was tasked to the National Defense Research Committee, or NDRC. The NDRC was conceived by renowned scientist Vannevar Bush. Seeing the signs that the United States would soon be mobilizing for war, and concerned about a disconnect between the nation's military and rapidly advancing science, Bush formulated a plan to create a committee to remedy this condition. On 12 June 1940 President Roosevelt approved Bush's proposal, and named Bush to head the NDRC.

One year and one day after the establishment of the NDRC, the structure of the organization would change. Executive Order 8807 was signed on 28 June 1941, establishing the Office of Scientific Research and Development (OSRD). Notable was the addition of 'and Development' in this organization's name, as compared to the National Defense Research Committee.

While the NDRC had originally been placed under the Council for National Defense, the OSRD was placed within the Office of Emergency Management of the Executive Office of the President. The Director of the OSRD would be appointed by, and report directly to, the President of the United States. Executive Order 8807 specifically moved the NDRC to the auspices of OSRD.

The shifting of the NDRC to being a unit of the OSRD resulted in the NDRC no longer having the authority to act itself, but merely to recommend action by the OSRD. The reorganized NDRC first met on 18 July 1941. One interesting aspect of both the NDRC and OSRD operations was the premise that research itself should be non-profit, whether conducted by an institution or university, or by commercial enterprise. Thus, the contracts used by NDRC/OSRD were structured so that those contracted would neither gain nor lose financially for the work. The various divisions of OSRD were tasked with projects divided by field, with Division 12 dealing with transportation matters.

President Roosevelt named Vannevar Bush as Director of Office of Scientific Research and Development. Bush, feeling he could not direct both OSRD and NDRC, appointed J.B. Conant as chairman of NDRC. Encompassing many of the country's top scientists, the NDRC, with its broad responsibilities, played a significant role in the US war effort. In addition to the Weasel, the NDRC was responsible for the development of the GPA amphibious jeep, the DUKW amphibious truck, proximity fuses – and even the early nuclear program.

Contrary to the often-seen images of military vehicles *pushing* their way through mud, the only effective way to operate in deep snow is to stay on top of it, and the only way to stay on top is by maintaining a low ground pressure. The US Army tested, and sometimes bought in limited quantities, a number of vehicles whose principal function was to operate over the top of snow; virtually all of these were track-laying vehicles. In some instances the army turned to manufacturers of civilian snow machines, such as Eliason and Tucker. Commercial machines were also adapted to military use. In other cases, military programs resulted in the refinement of some designs and the creation of totally new ones. Some were from established manufacturers of snow equipment, while others were the work of firms not normally associated with snow vehicles.

The latter was the case with the Studebaker-developed family of T15 and T24 cargo carriers, which went on to become the M28 and M29 vehicles, popularly known as Weasels.

The Weasel

The initial requirements for the vehicle that would become the Weasel stipulated that the new vehicle fit within the bomb bay of the British Lancaster bomber or inside a US glider, that it could be dropped by parachute onto bare lake ice and be able to drive away immediately after landing. While these specifications were later modified to include being suspended beneath a C-54, the requirements continued to include having good speed in snow, high maneuverability in forests, able to cross bare rocks and railroad tracks, and excellent performance on hills and sideslopes, all while laden with a 1,200 pound payload.

Despite the impressive list of requirements, since the vehicle was being designed for a specific mission – a mission that it was thought would entail average operation of 100 miles, 90 on snow and 10 on hard surfaces – the vehicle was required to have a life of only 1,000 miles. And, because it was intended for a specific mission, the NDRC was to see to it that within 180 days of being given the problem, production vehicles would be delivered.

Of course, to develop a snow vehicle, access to snow was important, despite it being summer time. Suitable snow was located in Soda Springs, California, and test personnel arrived there on 4 May 1942. Division 12 dubbed the new vehicle the Weasel, and on 17 May engineers at Studebaker, who had been contracted by OSRD, began on the pilot model designs.

The first pilot model, which in a precursor of things to come was amphibious, was completed in thirty-eight days. A second, non-amphibious pilot was also produced.

As the pilots neared completion, efforts were put into locating a suitable Proving Ground, offering abundant snow and some degree of secrecy. After an extensive evaluation of North and South America, the site selected was 400 square miles of the Columbia ice fields in Canada, 60 miles north of Lake Louise and 9,000 feet above sea level. The Canadian National Park Service built an access road, and the US Army and Studebaker built a Proving Ground. The 87th Mountain Infantry Regiment operated the camp.

The pilots were subjected to extensive tests, beginning in August 1942. Parachute tests were conducted at Wright Field, Ohio, and South Bend, Indiana.

The result of these tests was the finalization of the design which was designated T15. Because of the urgency of meeting the mission deadline, production tooling was being created even before the testing was complete. However, the planned operation in Norway was cancelled, and the schedule relaxed slightly, so the first production models did not roll off the South Bend assembly line until 205 days after the project began (vs the original 180-day timetable). The T15 was subsequently standardized as the M28.

As mentioned, the T15 was committed to production even before testing was complete. The further tests revealed several shortcomings in the design, and an improved model, the T24, was engineered to address many of those problems. The T24 offered increased life, reduced rolling resistance, improved engine-cooling, permitting operation in tropical areas, increased flotation and cargo capacity, and improved suspension and hill-climbing.

Testing of the new T24 vehicle, which differed from the T15 in having a front engine and rear drive, began in March 1943. The tests proved favorable, and the T24 was subsequently standardized as the M29.

However, the amphibious capability offered by the original prototype had not been forgotten, and in April 1943 tests began with a view to developing an amphibious version of the M29. The resulting vehicle, which had bow and stern flotation tanks, track guards to aid with in-water propulsion, twin rudders, and a capstan winch, was designated the M-29C. While the NDRC preferred the name 'Ark' for the M29C, in practice the vehicle retained the Weasel name of its predecessors.

The Weasels saw use in the Aleutians, Italy, France, Germany and most of the major island campaigns in the Pacific during the Second World War. Despite several attempts at developing follow-on vehicles, the Weasel was again fielded in Korea. Remarkably, there is photographic evidence of at least one of the venerable vehicles in service in south-east Asia in the 1960s.

One of the earliest snow vehicle designs tried by the Army was this Sno-Motor, designed and built during 1941 at the US Forest Service's Equipment Laboratory in Portland, Oregon. First sent to Camp McCoy, Wisconsin and later to Aberdeen Proving Ground for testing, the vehicle was not notably successful. As can be imagined, the vehicle's single track made for an unorthodox steering mechanism. A winch and cables were used to shift the towed sled from side to side in order to steer the vehicle. (TACOM LCMC History Office)

Above: Produced by Emmitt M. Tucker's Sno-Cat company, this T26 was one of six purchased by the army. At the time of this machine's delivery, Tucker had twenty years' experience designing snow vehicles. The powerplant of this vehicle was a four-cylinder liquid-cooled engine. (TACOM LCMC History Office)

Opposite above: Photographed during 1944 testing, the Tucker T26E1 Snow Tractor, powered by an air-cooled engine, showed considerable promise. It seated two people, in-line, and was of a half-track design. Its front wheels could be replaced with skis for operation in deep snow. (TACOM LCMC History Office)

Opposite below: Curiously, this photo bears the same date and location as the other view of the T26E1, yet there are considerable differences in the two vehicles – and weather! The road wheels are mounted externally on this example and headlamps have been installed. A tarpaulin protects the crew cabin. (TACOM LCMC History Office)

Above: The T26E3 retained the basic layout of its predecessors, but now the return track run was flat rather than peaked, and the engine type reverted to liquid-cooled. The cabin has been extended slightly over the tracks, which are now notably carried by an open-type suspension system. (TACOM LCMC History Office)

Opposite above: Further development led to the installation of the four-cylinder Willys engine, as used in the MB and GPW Jeeps. Also adapted from the Jeep was the rear axle, although it was shortened on the T26E4. As compared to the T26E3, the suspension was increased from three road wheels to five. This T26E4 is being loaded into the bed of a CCKW after a round of testing. (TACOM LCMC History Office)

Opposite below: The T26E4 – shown here during September 1943 Aberdeen Proving Ground testing – was envisioned as a rescue vehicle, primarily for downed flyers. The tractor itself had room only for the driver and one passenger. Thus, the M19 one-ton trailer was developed. Mounting either wheels or skis, the M19 could accommodate an attendant and two litter-borne patients, in the relative comfort of an insulated enclosure equipped with a gas-fired heater. (National Archives)

The M19 trailer was provided with a rear-mounted pintle hook, allowing the tractor to pull a train of these trailers. The trailer was also equipped to house an aircraft engine warmer, a necessity for operating aircraft from bitterly cold bases. (National Archives)

Ultimately, the T26E4 was standardized as the M7. Some 291 of these machines were produced by Allis-Chalmers, ranking it along with the Weasel as the only specialized snow vehicle mass-produced for the military during the Second World War. The first 100 or so were equipped with bronze axle housings, while the balance used conventional castings, again adapted from Jeep units. Brakes were adapted from those of Harley-Davidson motorcycles. Note the insulated cover for the engine compartment, and the unpainted contact surfaces of the skis, shown here stowed and acting as front fenders. (TACOM LCMC History Office)

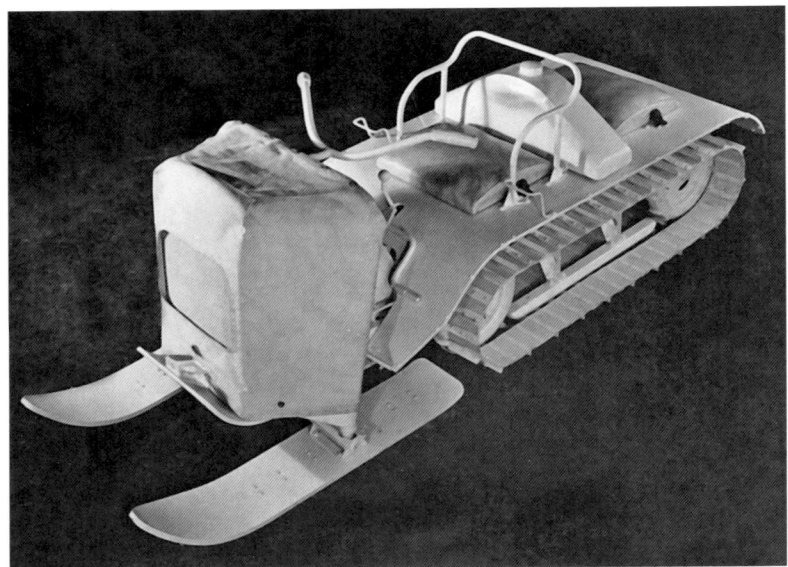

Seaman Motor Company of Milwaukee produced the T27, a snowmobile-like vehicle. This effort was refined and the T27E1 Snow Tractor created. Seaman delivered one of the T27E1, while Allis-Chalmers built eleven more. The machine, considerably smaller than the M7, was powered by an air-cooled engine. (TACOM LCMC History Office)

Allis-Chalmers also built the T27E2, an improved model with an extended engine compartment. Separating the driver from the passenger was the fuel tank. Like the T27 and T27E1, the vehicle was steered via handlebars that turned the skis. (TACOM LCMC History Office)

The four Crosley T28 snow tractors were truly motorized toboggans, with a simple wood sled covering the entire bottom of the vehicle. An open-frame track circumscribed the entire unit, pulling it, and its standing operator, along. Mounting points were provided at the front, allowing the T28 to push, rather than pull, its payload. (TACOM LCMC History Office)

Four T28E1 tractors were also built by Crosley. Once tested successfully, serious consideration was given to placing this unit in mass production. It differed from its predecessor by incorporating two parallel-running conventional track belts. This improved both steering and flotation. Power for the T28 and T28E1 was provided by a 35cid, 12hp Crosley air-cooled opposed-cylinder engine.

The versatile Jeep was tried as a specialized snow vehicle. Adapted from one of the TUG 6x6 variants, the T29 had a non-driven front axle at the front and tracks at the rear. The two leading road wheels were mounted on a walking beam to ensure continuous track tension when crossing undulating terrain. (TACOM LCMC History Office)

International Harvester further refined the T29 design, resulting in the T29E1. Six of these vehicles were tested at Camp Hale, Colorado, in 1943. The small contact area of the front skis, compared to the contact area of the tracks, and combined with the soft, slippery snow, made the vehicle difficult to steer and the project was ultimately abandoned. (TACOM LCMC History Office)

The Alaska Highway was operated by the Army for the duration, and provided a location for testing of winter gear within the relative safety of the North American continent. Here an Eliason Motor Toboggan is being tested in January 1944. Eliason was the developer of what is now known as the snowmobile, and during the Second World War the company was owned by the FWD Auto Company of Clintonville, WI. (TACOM LCMC History Office)

Crosley also built the unusual-looking T30. Looking more like a First World War-era artillery tractor than a 1944 snow tractor, little is known about this vehicle, though six were built. Continually refined, the design became known as the Crosley Mule, and culminated in the T37 light tractor. (TACOM LCMC History Office)

The large orange vehicle in the background is the T36 snow tractor. The Army purchased thirty-six of these during 1944, each powered by a Dodge T-214 engine. Equipped with a three-man cab, twelve-volt electrical system and SCR-187 radio, the vehicle proved to be reasonably successful. Little known as a vehicle manufacturer, the Iron Fireman Company – a noted maker of coal stoker screws – made a brief entry into the vehicle field, including the T36. (Denver Public Library)

CHAPTER 1

The T15/M24

On 1 May 1942, General Marshall asked Dr Vannevar Bush, Director of Office of Scientific Research and Development, to develop a snow-traversing vehicle to be utilized in Operation Plough. The UK Prime Minister's mission had requested a vehicle that would 'literally convert snow from a barrier into a highway'. The vehicle was to be able to operate on snow, mud, rocks, dry land and water – and was to be air-transportable. The requirement was for the vehicle to be transportable in a glider, or delivered by air-dropping from a Lancaster bomber. Not only that, the vehicle was to be able to move out under its own power immediately after landing. Adding to these already heavy demands, the delivery of the first 600 production vehicles should begin in 180 days.

Bush assigned the project to the NDRC's Division 12, whose responsibilities included communication and, appropriately, transportation. Division 12 was to work directly with the Assistant Chief of Staff, G-4, War Department General Staff.

Added to the requirements laid out previously, the new vehicle was to have a cargo capacity of 1,200 pounds. On the plus side, from the design standpoint, since this vehicle was designed specifically for Operation Plough, each vehicle was expected to average less than 100 miles – 90 on snow and 10 on harder surfaces. Thus the design criteria required a vehicle life of only 1,000 miles.

As the required vehicle would be pioneering in many regards, little prior engineering knowledge existed. This obstacle was compounded because the deadline established was 180 days – from the first of May. It was estimated that 130 of those days would be required to create the tooling for production – and forty for engineering and producing the experimental and pilot models. This meant snow had to be found for testing in July.

By 4 May snow had been located in Soda Springs, California, and scientists and engineers began studying the snow, and the operation of existing snow vehicles, with special emphasis on the interaction between vehicle and snow. Of the existing snow vehicles, the two that most nearly met the new requirements were the Bombardier snowmobile and the Army Air Force's M7 snow tractor. Both of these vehicles, as well as all the others with front skis, were found to have difficulty making turns at high speeds, especially when running downhill. In addition to the half-track/half-ski vehicles, also tested was a Jeep fitted with 17.00x20 airplane tires, fully tracked vehicles, and vehicles driven by Archimedian screws.

The researchers soon realized that vastly more knowledge about snow itself, and the various types of snow, would be required in order to design an effective vehicle. Regardless, it was also quickly determined that ground pressure should be kept to a minimum, but could not be too low as that would adversely affect steering. By 17 May, work had begun on the design of the pilot vehicle, and the name Weasel had been chosen for it.

Studebaker, a noted car manufacturer based in South Bend, Indiana, was selected to produce the fully-tracked vehicle, which would be driven by sprockets on the forward end of the vehicle. The engine and powertrain were essentially standard automotive items, with which Studebaker was well familiar. They were to be enclosed in a simple hull. What remained was to design adequate suspension as well as track.

In only thirty-eight days a pilot model, which was amphibious, had been completed. It rode on eight bogie wheels arranged in four pairs on each side. Tipping the scales at 7,000 pounds, the midships-engined machine could carry a crew of two, with stowage space in the hull sponsons. Propulsion in the water was via a PTO-driven propeller. Lacking a rudder, testing proved that steering in water was difficult, verging on impossible.

An additional, non-amphibious pilot was designed, and four examples hand-built. As these were being built, representatives of Division 12 sought a proving ground for extensive testing that would also meet the security needs demanded by the secret mission. After clandestinely investigating mountainous regions in South America and Alaska, it was finally decided that Canada's Columbia ice fields would be appropriate. Encompassing 400 square miles 60 miles north of Lake Louise and 9,000 feet above sea level, the area was so remote that the Canadian National Park Service had to build a road to the snout of the glacier. The US Army and Studebaker constructed a camp, which was operated by the 87th Mountain Infantry Regiment. Testing began in earnest in August.

The disadvantage of the remote locale was that when parts failed during testing, or tests indicated a redesign was required, the new components had to be flown in, requiring at a minimum 36 hours.

Due to the extreme urgency of the situation, tooling for the production vehicles began long before the testing of the pilot models was completed. Before production actually began, Operation Plough had been cancelled, affording a little more time. Nonetheless, the first production models were complete 205 days after the project began. The vehicle was standardized as the M28.

With the cancellation of Operation Plough, the T15 saw combat service in only one significant operation – the recapture of Kiska in the Aleutian Islands. While in the snow the T15 performed better than the other vehicles, attempts to use the vehicles on rocky beaches resulted in destroyed tracks. The T15 was also used for training purposes by the 10th Mountain Division at Camp Hale, and by the AAF Arctic Training Center in Colorado.

Studebaker developed the Light Cargo Carrier T15 in 1942 as part of a special project to supply the First Special Service Force with a cargo vehicle capable of operating on snow for a projected campaign in Norway later that year. This is the first pilot T15. (Patton Museum)

Above: A T15 or its production version, M28, is being hoisted above the deck of an unidentified troopship in April 1943. The view is from the rear of the vehicle. The cambered bogie wheels are apparent. On top of the sponson are two racks for stowing skis. (National Archives)

Opposite above: The T15 had provisions for a driver, a passenger behind the driver, and stowage for skis, a radio, snowshoes, and other essentials for operating in wintry conditions. In this overhead view with the top removed, the front of the T15 is to the right. (Patton Museum)

Opposite below: Studebaker received the request to design the T15 in May 1942. Here, a T15 is shown in a photo dated 29 August 1942. Various designs of drive wheels and idler wheels were experimented with. The ones shown here had holes in them to prevent ice build-up. (Patton Museum)

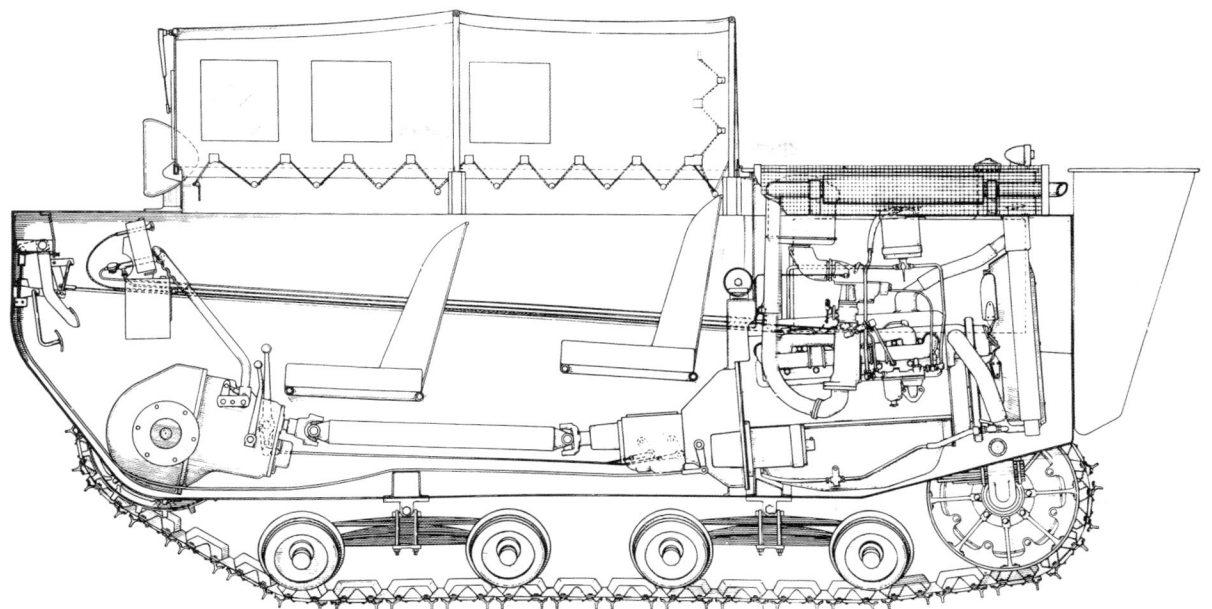

Above: The rear-engine, front-drive arrangement of the T15 is clearly illustrated in this vintage cross-sectional drawing.

Opposite above: Two Light Cargo Carriers T15 involved in maneuvers have their serial numbers stenciled on the hull front. Both vehicles have a camouflage scheme of white with black applied in splotches and streaks. The carrier to the left is marked 502 and the one to the right 581. (National Archives)

Opposite below: A T15 is used as a tractor to tow a number of cargo-bearing sleds on a 15-mile move at the Camp James Lake area of Camp Crowder, Michigan, on 5 March 1945. This is the HQ Company of the 38th Infantry Regiment, and the temperature was 20 below zero when this scene was captured. (National Archives)

The Studebaker Light Cargo Carrier T15 Weasel, later standardized as the Light Cargo Carrier M28, was designed to be air-transportable and to operate on snow and ice. It had a top speed of 35 miles per hour and a cargo capacity of 1,260 pounds. The Military Vehicle Preservation Group of Spooner, Wisconsin, restored this Light Cargo Carrier T15. It was assigned Ordnance serial number 184. Archival photos indicate that typically, registration numbers (which in this case are spurious) were not stenciled on the outside of T15 carriers.

On the M28, the sponsons were tapered, with their height being taller at the rear than at the front. To protect the crew from the elements, a canvas top with soft-plastic windows was provided, supported by the windshield frame and two bows. The tracks were a flexible-cable, band-type design, with the drive wheels mounted on the front of the chassis and powered by a controlled differential.

The left drive wheel is shown close-up. Attached to the inner perimeter of the tracks on each side is an endless chain. A thin rubber tire is on each rim of the drive wheel. To each side of the track guide is a rubber band, which lends flexibility to the track. The addition of chain or cable to the track is a common repair by vehicle enthusiasts, but is not an original military or Studebaker feature.

Above: Four bogies are on each side of the T15. The bogies are mounted in pairs, one on each end of a compound elliptical-spring assembly, which comprises three sets of springs stacked one on top of the other. At the upper center is a guide wheel.

Below: The bogie wheels of the Light Cargo Carrier T15 were cambered, with the bottoms of the wheels angled toward the center of the track. This design was intended to reduce the frequency of thrown tracks, a problem with vertically oriented wheels.

The compound elliptical springs of the T15 are mounted on outriggers (top) that jut from the sides of the hull. At the front and at the rear of the elliptical spring assembly is an axle on which the dual bogie wheels are mounted.

In addition to being cambered, the bogie wheels of the Light Cargo Carrier T15 were designed to swivel longitudinally on the axles up to 26 degrees. This allowed the tracks to flex to a significant degree before a thrown track could result.

The left side of the suspension is viewed from underneath the T15. Each bogie wheel included two outer disks with rubber tires and two inner disks with no tires. Grousers are affixed to the outer sides of the track shoes for added traction.

On each side of the rear of the T15 is a track-idler wheel. The idler-wheel carrier, which included the axle, was connected to the leaf spring visible on the side of the hull to the front of the idler wheel. V-section grousers are visible on the track.

The left track is viewed from the rear. During the development of the T15 prototype, several types of tracks were experimented with, including one of woven-wire mesh design, and this type with two molded rubber bands with steel cross members and track shoes.

The Light Cargo Carrier T15 Weasel of the Military Vehicle Preservation Group of Spooner, Wisconsin, is viewed from the left rear. At the upper center rear of the hull is the air-duct door in the open position. The engine of the T15 faces to the rear, and the radiator is just forward of the air-duct door. To each side of that door is a stowage compartment with a door and a clamp-type latch on top.

At the lower center of the rear of the hull is a pintle hook for towing a sled. The hook is situated on a cast bracket fastened to the lower rear plate of the hull. The feature at the top center is the cover for the manual engine start crank.

More of the rear of the T15 is shown. The grousers were permanently mounted on the track shoes. The ones here are V-shaped in profile, with a scalloped edge, the better to dig into icy surfaces. A square opening is at the center of each shoe.

The Light Cargo Carrier T15 is observed from the right side. A coaming, raised above the deck of the hull, surrounds the crew compartment and the engine compartment. Mounted on the side of the rear of the coaming is a blackout marker lamp. The cover over the engine compartment is fitted with clamp latches. Two brackets on the deck hold cross-country skis and ski poles. At the front of the hull is the headlight assembly and brush guard.

The guide wheels have thin rubber tires that bear on the continuous rubber bands of the tracks. The track guides pass through the gap between the paired wheels. Below the rollers, details of the construction of the bogie outrigger are visible.

The right front guide wheels are shown. To the far right are the sprockets of the right drive wheel.

The hubcap of the guide wheel is fastened with four slotted screws. On military tracked vehicles, this wheel usually is referred to as a track-return roller or a track-support roller, but official reports on the T15 referred to them as guide wheels.

A set of guide wheels is viewed from the front, showing the shaft between the two wheels. The rubber bands that form the longitudinal supports for the tracks are fastened to the track shoes with large rivets through metal tabs.

The right drive wheel is viewed from the rear. At the center are the two sprockets. The rest of the rims of the wheels are covered with thin rubber tires. The rubber on these wheels is vintage and heavily cracked. To the left is the carrier assembly.

Above: The front end of the T15 belonging to the Military Vehicle Preservation Group of Spooner, Wisconsin, is viewed from the right side. The vehicle has one headlight, on the left side of the forward deck. A tow eye is on the front of the hull. (John Adams-Graf)

Opposite: The Light Cargo Carrier T15 is observed from the front right. The sponsons above the tracks are noticeably tapered, with the high end being situated to the rear. On the M29 Weasel, this would be reversed, with the high end to the front. (John Adams-Graf)

Above: On the deck to the front of the windshield are two raised brackets fitted with clamps for securing the windshield in the 'down' position. On the deck to the side of the driver's compartment are two brackets for stowing a .30-caliber BAR inside a canvas cover. An M1919 will also fit, when laid on its side (rather than upright). A tow eye is on the front of the hull.

Opposite above: In a view of the lower front of the hull of the T15, the metal fittings at the corners of the hull were guards to prevent debris from fouling the tracks. Along the lower center of the hull the seam between the two hull bottom halves is visible. (John Adams-Graf)

Opposite below: The windshield assembly of the T15 consists of a frame, hinged at the bottom; a single pane of glass; a brace on each side connected to the rear of the frame; and windshield wipers and electric motor. An aiming handle is on top of the spotlight case. (John Adams-Graf)

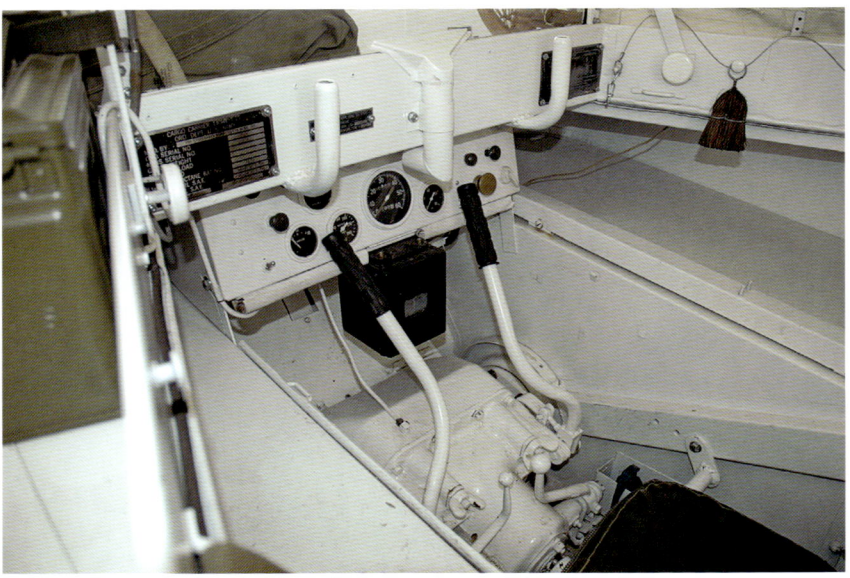

A mast base for a radio antenna is on the deck to the left side of the driver's compartment of this T15. To the front of the antenna is a Browning air-cooled .30-caliber machine gun, stowed on two brackets attached to the deck. A tow eye is on the front of the hull.

In the driver's compartment, to the front is the instrument panel, with a compass below it and the two steering levers to the rear of the instrument panel. To the bottom right is the front right corner of the driver's seat. This vehicle is missing the asbestos heat cover over the differential and does not have the covers on the side stowage areas of the insides. (Rick Forys)

On the left of the front coaming is a nomenclature plate identifying this vehicle as a Light Cargo Carrier T15, Ordnance serial number 184. The plate gives specifications for the fuel octane, 70 to 72, and oil: SAE 30 in summer and SAE 10 in winter.

On the right side of the driver's compartment is stowage space. The right brace of the windshield is attached at the bottom to the inside of the coaming. To the right of center, a bow is inserted into a socket on the coaming, to support the canvas top.

This is a driver's-eye view of the driving controls and the instrument panel of a T15. The small data plate to the right of the nomenclature plate is a list of manuals for the vehicle. On the coaming to the right is a plate with shifting instructions.

The driver's compartment of a T15 is observed from the right. Between the steering levers are the transmission shift lever and the shifter for the axle gear box, a two-speed unit with a high and a low range. The axle gear box is the mechanism on the floor. (Rob Walsh)

The passenger's seat is to the rear of the driver's seat, over the longitudinal centerline of the T15. The seat is mounted on a frame that rests on cup-shaped holders fastened to the hull, for easy removability. As manufactured, all of the canvas items on the T15 were white rather than Olive Drab. The drive shaft runs through the area below the seat. (Rob Walsh)

In the T15 and standardized T28 there was room for only one seat in the passenger's compartment to the rear of the driver's seat. The top of the passenger's seat is to the left in this view facing aft; to the lower right is a radio set, and a helmet is on top of it.

The Light Cargo Carrier T15 is observed from above and to the rear. The cover of the ventilation air duct is in the closed position at the center rear of the hull. Snowshoes are stowed on top of the engine-compartment cover. Pioneer tools are stowed to the front of the snowshoes. To the left of the engine compartment is a screen-type guard over the muffler. (John Adams-Graf)

The muffler guard, left, is viewed from the rear. To the rear of the muffler is a short tailpipe. To the right is the cover for the engine compartment; it is hinged at the front, and one of two latch handles for the cover is in the right foreground.

The muffler guard is fabricated of woven steel wire with a reinforcing strip at each end. The tailpipe protrudes from the rear of the guard. At the upper right, the cover for the air duct is in the open position. To the right is a stowage container.

In keeping with the T15's purpose as a vehicle for operating in snowy climes, a stack of snowshoes is strapped to the top of the engine-compartment cover. Footman loops, for attaching straps for securing cargo, are welded to the engine-compartment cover.

The engine compartment of the T15 is observed from the rear. Powering the T15 was the Studebaker Model 6-170 Champion, an inline, six-cylinder, four-cycle engine with a displacement of 169.6 cubic inches. This engine had a brake horsepower of 75. (Rick Forys)

At the upper left is the air cleaner. The gray canister at the upper center is the oil-diluter tank assembly. The dark-colored canister partially visible behind the oil-diluter tank is the oil filter. To the lower left is the battery. Wartime engines were painted in heat-resistant gray rather than green. (Rick Forys)

The carburetor on the Studebaker Model 6-170 engine is the brownish assembly at the center of the photo. To the upper right is the radiator, located at the rear of the engine compartment. To the upper left is the open cover of the engine compartment. (Rick Forys)

Opening the hinged cover of the air ventilation duct at the rear of the hull of the T15 facilitated air movement through the radiator. The cover is shown in the open position. A dark-colored gasket serves as a seal around the inner perimeter of the top of the duct.

A compartment for stowing cargo and equipment is on each side of the air ventilation duct on the rear of the T15. The lid of the stowage compartment on the right is viewed from the rear. The lid is equipped with a hold-down clamp secured to a bracket. The main purpose of these stowage compartments was to add buoyancy to the vehicle. While the T-15 was not optimized for amphibious operation as was the later M29C, it was intended to float.

At the right rear of the engine-compartment cover of the Light Cargo Carrier T15 is the fuel filler cap. Below it on the right side of the engine compartment is the fuel tank. In the right foreground is the right hold-down clamp for the engine-compartment cover.

A blackout marker lamp is at the right rear corner of the coaming around the engine compartment. Blackout marker lamps were designed to make the vehicle visible to other nearby, friendly drivers without disclosing the location of the vehicle to the enemy.

The design of the rear of the canvas top over the driver's and passenger's compartments of the T15 is displayed. Two soft-plastic windows are incorporated into the rear curtain. Also in view are pioneer tools: a shovel and a mattock handle, strapped to a lid.

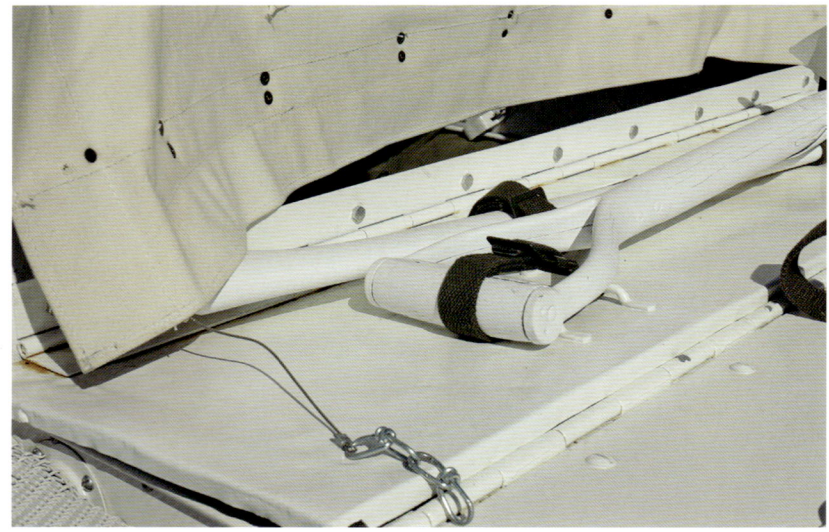

The lid that the pioneer tools are strapped to is hinged at the front and can be raised to allow airflow through a duct below it. That hinge runs across the center of the photo. To the lower right is the hinge at the front of the cover of the engine compartment.

Brackets or racks for carrying cross-country skis and ski poles were standard equipment on the right side of the deck of the Light Cargo Carrier T15. The brackets, as viewed from the front, were fastened to the deck with screws and hex nuts.

The front ski rack is shown with a pair of skis and poles stowed on it. The inboard upright of the bracket is welded to the base plate, while the bottom of the outboard upright is hinged. The tops of the uprights are connected with a pin and cotter pin.

The spotlight assembly is viewed from the right rear. The spotlight is enclosed in a dome-shaped housing. A hoop-shaped handle is welded to the housing. To the front of the headlight assembly is a brush guard. To the rear of the light is the power cord.

The spotlight assembly is observed from the front. Its round base plate is fastened to the deck with four hex screws. To the lower right is the right clamp for securing the windshield in the lowered position. A wing nut is on the outboard side of the clamp.

CHAPTER 2

The T24/M29

The track and suspension of the T15 had high rolling resistance and contributed to rough operation, and the life of the tracks suffered due to the small rivets used in its construction. However, the low ground pressure of the vehicle made it well suited for use in swamps and mud. To address the shortcomings and increase the versatility of the Weasel, a complete redesign was initiated.

Track width was increased to 20 inches, the drive sprockets were made smaller and were moved to the rear, and the engine was moved to the front, shifting the center of gravity to 52 inches forward of the centerline. A completely new suspension system was engineered using sixteen bogie wheels. The resulting vehicle, the T24, showed marked improvements during tests. In addition to lower rolling resistance, the T24 had improved gas mileage, a better ride, could climb better and had increased cargo space, now being capable of holding twice as many people as the T15.

Production of the new vehicle, which was eventually standardized as the M29, began on 30 August 1943.

Opposite above: The Cargo Carrier M29 was noticeably different in design from the T15/M28, with more bogie wheels, arranged vertically; different suspension and tracks; and sponsons that were higher at the front than at the rear. This example is viewed from the front right. (Patton Museum)

Opposite below: The same M29 shown in the preceding photo, Ordnance serial number 2581, is observed in a 17 March 1944 photo from the right rear with the top removed. This example had a radio antenna mount on a frame that straddled the muffler guard on the rear deck. (Patton Museum)

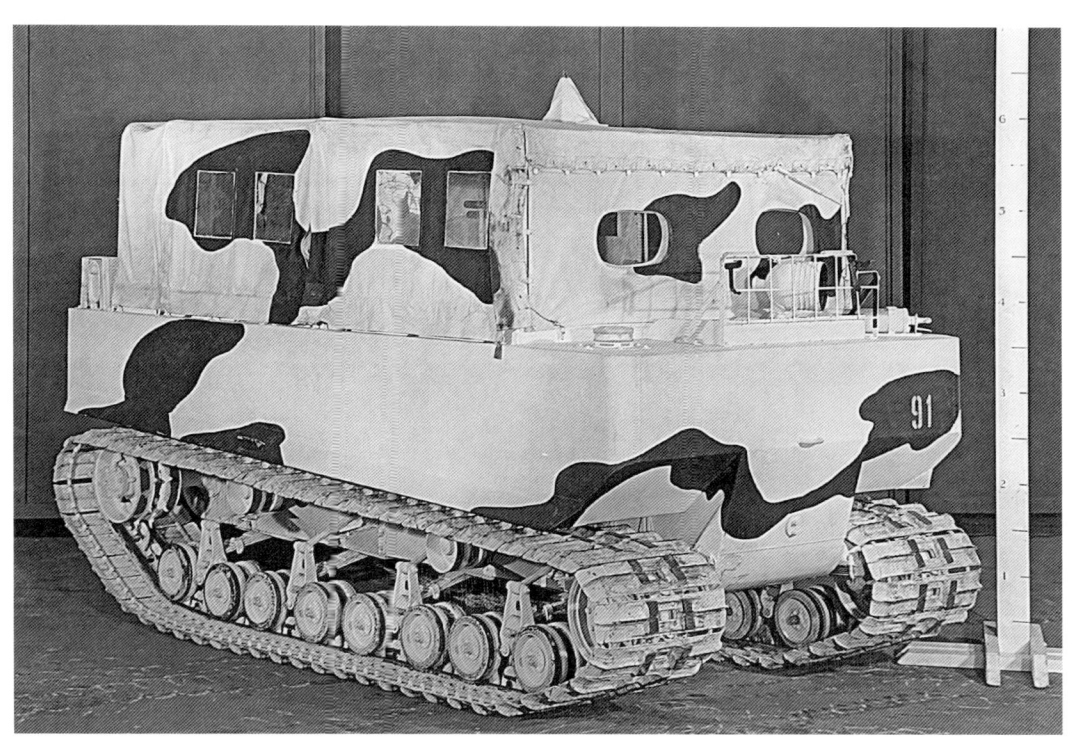

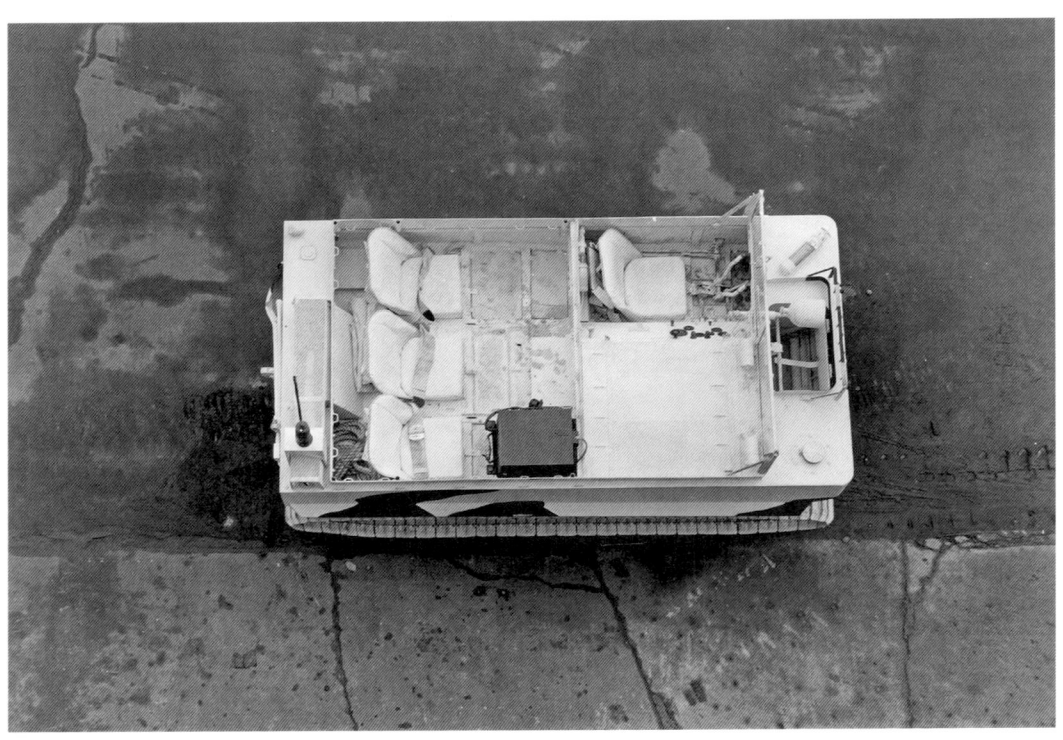

Above: The Light Cargo Carrier T24 was an improved development of the Light Cargo Carrier T15/ M28. Studebaker produced a total of 1,002 units of the T24 in 1943. The T24 was standardized as the Light Cargo Carrier M29. Whereas the Light Cargo Carrier T15/M28 carried only two persons, the T24 carried up to four persons. The T24 was designed to operate on difficult terrain, deep snow, mud, and in combat zones.

Opposite above: An overhead view portrays the layout and features of the same M29 shown on page 35. The driver sat in the left front, with the engine compartment to his right. To the rear was a passenger compartment with three individual seats. A radio is to the front right of that compartment. (Patton Museum)

Opposite below: M29 Ordnance serial number 2581 is observed from the left rear of the passengers' compartment. To the upper right is a radio set on a frame-type holder. A handset is on the left side of the radio. The driver's compartment and instrument panel are at the top left. (Patton Museum)

Above: In the T24, the driver's compartment is on the left side of the vehicle; three side-by-side seats are available for passengers. The sides of the sponsons are tapered, with the higher end of the sponsons to the front. Eight dual bogie wheels are on each side.

Opposite above: In addition to having the taller ends of the sponsons to the front, the fronts of the T24's sponsons featured angled lower facets, a characteristic not present on the T15/M24 carriers. The T24 had a larger effective area of track in ground contact than the T15/M28.

Opposite below: The T24 suspension included idler wheels at the front, drive wheels at the rear, two guide wheels, and eight pairs of bogie wheels on each side, vertically oriented, not cambered as on the T15/M24.

Above: On the front deck is a coaming around the air duct for the radiator. Situated in the left front corner of the duct is a mount for a headlight that doubled as a removable spotlight. U-shaped rests for the windshield when lowered are on the front corners of the deck.

Opposite above: On the front of the hull of the T24 is a large brushguard. It could be installed in two configurations: fastened to the front of the deck for maximum height, or fastened to two small brackets on the front of the hull, as shown here, for a lower profile. (John Adams-Graf)

Opposite below: Here, the brushguard is installed on the deck of the T24, with a brace on each side extending back to the side of the air-duct coaming. On the vertical front plate of the hull are the two small brackets for stowing the brushguard in the lowered position.

On the T24 a spotlight extended through the driver's windshield just above the left side of the radiator. It could be aimed forward to act as a headlight during night operations. (John Adams-Graf)

The fuel-filler neck and cap on the T24 were near the front right corner of the front deck, with a flange on the neck being affixed to the deck with hex screws and washers. The fuel filler would remain in the same location relative to the radiator air duct through the M29 and M29C.

With the high aspect of the fronts of the sponsons, the raised coaming around the hatch on the front deck, and the eight sets of dual bogie wheels, the Light Cargo Carrier T24 was noticeably different from its predecessor, the Light Cargo Carrier T15/M28.

The left track of a Cargo Carrier T24 is viewed from the front end of the vehicle. Grousers were built into the track shoes and extend laterally across the center of the shoes. The grousers have a wavy edge, which made them more resistant to bending.

While the T15 was driven at the front of the track, the T24 was rear drive, making this steel wheel purely an idler.

The bogie wheels are mounted on four suspension units per side, featuring a leaf spring attached to the bottom of the hull on one side and to a support yoke on the outboard side. At the bottom of the yoke is a pivoting arm with twin bogie wheels on each end.

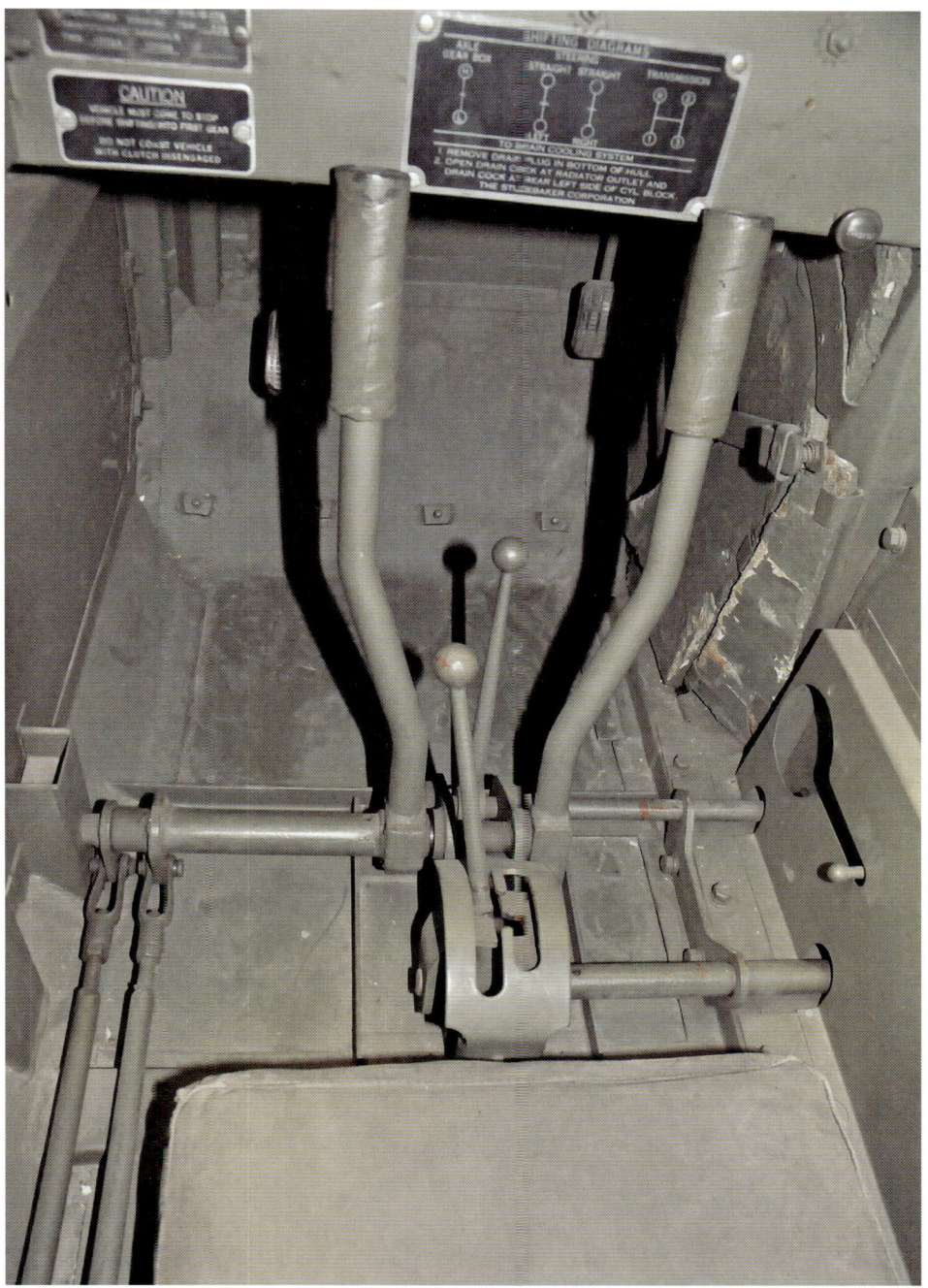

To the front of the driver's seat are the steering levers. The small lever between and to the front of the steering levers is the axle shift lever, to the rear of which is the transmission shift lever. The instrument panel is out of view to the right. Original seat covers were OD canvas on the T24 and white canvas on the T15. (Chris Hughes)

Above: The 18 bolts visible in the lower sides of this vehicle identify it as a T24. Another identifier is the lack of a flare above the track.

Opposite above: The large black knob that controls the aim of the spotlight is visible just beneath the windshield and to the right of the white-painted grab handle in this T24. (John Adams-Graf)

Opposite below: Camouflage netting is piled in the passenger compartment of a T24. In the center foreground is the vehicle's nomenclature and data plate. The objects with coil springs protruding from the top of the bulkhead in the foreground are hangers for stretchers. (John Adams-Graf)

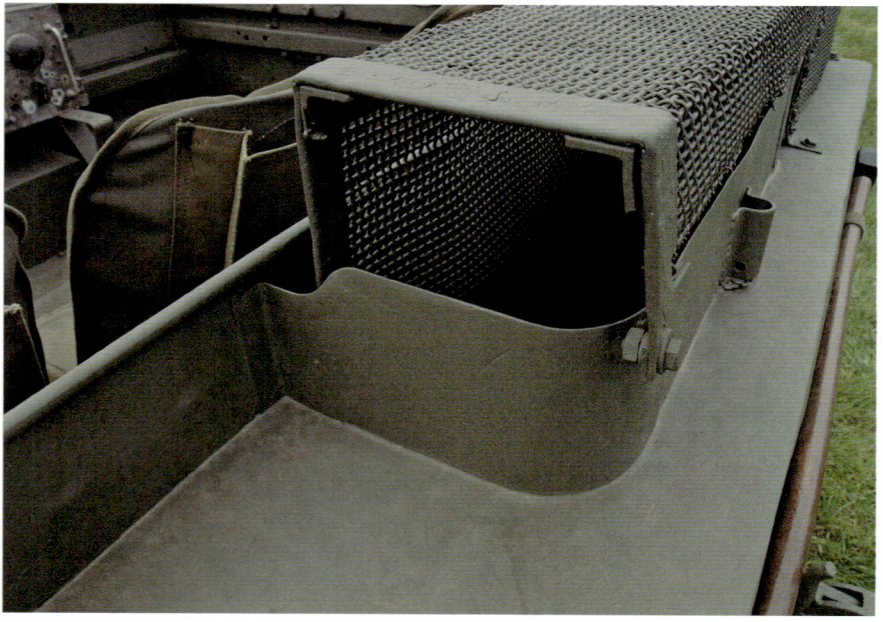

A different type of mast base is installed on the left side of the rear deck of this T24. To the lower left is a blackout marker lamp, intended to alert nearby drivers to the presence of this vehicle at night without disclosing the position of the vehicle to enemy observers.

At the center of the rear deck of the T24 is a well through which the exhaust pipe comes up from the bottom of the hull to join the muffler. A guard formed of woven steel wire and a steel frame covers this well, along with the muffler in the background. Engine cooling air is drawn through the front hatch, past the radiator and engine and is exhausted through this well and past the exhaust pipe.

Webbing straps through footman loops help secure the pioneer tools. The original small, rotating pintle hook on this vehicle has been replaced with a stationary, non-swiveling type, bolted to a steel plate that is bolted to the rear of the hull. This work was in accordance with a Modification Work Order.

The canvas top and left side curtain of a Cargo Carrier T24 are protecting the interior of this vehicle from the elements. The side curtain is in two pieces, with two plastic windows per panel. A canvas flap was provided near the center of the top, through which the radio antenna could extend on vehicles equipped with them.

A Cargo Carrier T24 is viewed from the right rear, showing the arrangement of the muffler guard and the coaming around the well where the exhaust line exits the hull.

The muffler guard is observed from adjacent to the right rear of the passenger compartment. The steel frame that reinforces the edge of the guard is bolted to the deck. The footman loops and the studs on the coaming are for securing a canvas curtain.

Features in the space to the rear of the passenger seats are displayed. Attached to the rear of each seat is a canvas stowage pouch with expanding-action sides and a webbing retainer strap at the top with a metal buckle. In the far corner is a spotlight. The sloping plate at the center of the rear bulkhead is removable and provides access to the differential and axle unit.

The seat-bottom cushions are removable and are secured with canvas straps, front and rear, that snap onto studs on the floor. The raised floor pan with the ribbing on it is removable to allow access to mechanical components in the lower part of the hull.

Above: The right front corner of the passenger compartment. Studs and footman loops for securing canvas side curtains are arranged along the inside of the coaming to the right. To the front is the cover of the engine compartment, the right half of which slants down.

Opposite above: To add to the strength of the seat hold-down system, the straps on the cushions pass under footman loops before being snapped onto the studs on the floor. The floor sections to each side of the removable floor pan were not designed to be removed.

Opposite below: The Weasel cargo carriers could mount a variety of radio sets, large and small, utilizing different types of racks in the passenger compartment. One such set and radio rack are shown here. The radio and rack straddles the rack for carrying demolition gear.

Above: In the suspension, there are four semi-elliptical springs that pass through the hull, serving two bogie assemblies, on opposite sides. A rod-shaped arm is connected to a bracket on the hull and the top of the yoke that supports the arms and bearings for the bogie wheels.

Opposite above: Between the hull and the drive wheel is the carrier assembly. The drive wheels, axle shafts and carriers can be removed as a unit by removing the hex screws on the rim of the carrier. This carrier and drive wheel unit is on the right rear of the hull of the T24.

Opposite below: Sandwiched between the two rims of the right drive wheel is the sprocket, with the teeth of the sprocket in alignment with the spokes of the wheels. Also in view is the outboard steel reinforcing cable of the track and the track guides between the rubber belts.

Above: A leaf spring and the arm linking the top of the bogie yoke to the bracket on the hull are in view. This mechanism allows the bogie units to flex upward and downward to conform to the terrain. A horizontal weld seam is on the hull in line with the arm bracket.

Opposite above: The bracket fastened to the side of the hull at the center of the photo supports one of the two sets of dual guide wheels found on each side of the Cargo Carrier T24. To the left and the lower right of the photo are two of the yokes of the bogie assemblies.

Opposite below: The guide wheels have thin rubber tires around their rims, and these tires make contact with the two continuous rubber belts that run around the inner perimeter of each track. The track guides at the center of the track pass through the gap between the guide wheels.

Above: Some of the bogie wheels and suspension assemblies are viewed from underneath the front of a T24. To the far left are the idler wheel and its carrier, which is in the form of a crank arm and which is attached with U-bolts to the leaf spring alongside the hull.

Opposite above: Weasels were sometimes called on to evacuate ill or wounded troops, and they were fitted with fixtures for mounting stretchers. This Cargo Carrier M29 has a stretcher with a dummy patient secured over the engine and the right side of the passenger compartment.

Opposite below: A canvas top is installed on this M29. The view is of the windshield from the left side. Inward-pointing metal tabs on the windshield serve to secure a metal cable running through sewn loops on the edges of the canvas top, thus holding this part of the top. (Chris Hughes)

This Cargo Carrier T24 with the canvas top and rear curtain installed and the side curtains folded in is owned and restored by Rick Wark. This vehicle lacks the splashguard along the bottom of the sponson. The shapes of the cable-retainer loops on the front edge of the top are visible. On the forward deck are the fuel filler cap, the coaming for the radiator air duct, and the headlight.

To provide clearance for the manually operated windshield wiper at the top of the left side of the windshield, the retainer loops for the cable on the front edge of the canvas top are cut in a V-shape, which fits over the shaft attached to the arm of the wiper. (Chris Hughes)

Above: Some of the loops and the steel retainer cable of the canvas top are viewed close-up at the upper left corner of the windshield. The hooks on the windshield frame that serve as catches for the steel cable have rounded ends and are cupped, for added strength. (Chris Hughes)

Opposite above: The provisions for securing the canvas top to the windshield are shown along the upper left edge of the windshield. To the right is the V-shaped cutout to provide space around the shaft and arm of the windshield wiper. Stitching the top was labor-intensive. (Chris Hughes)

Opposite below: In a view of the interior of the passenger compartment from the right side, the rear curtain is shown with its two soft-plastic windows. Fasteners are present for joining the curtain to the top. Two of the tubular metal bows that support the top and the curtains are in view. (Chris Hughes)

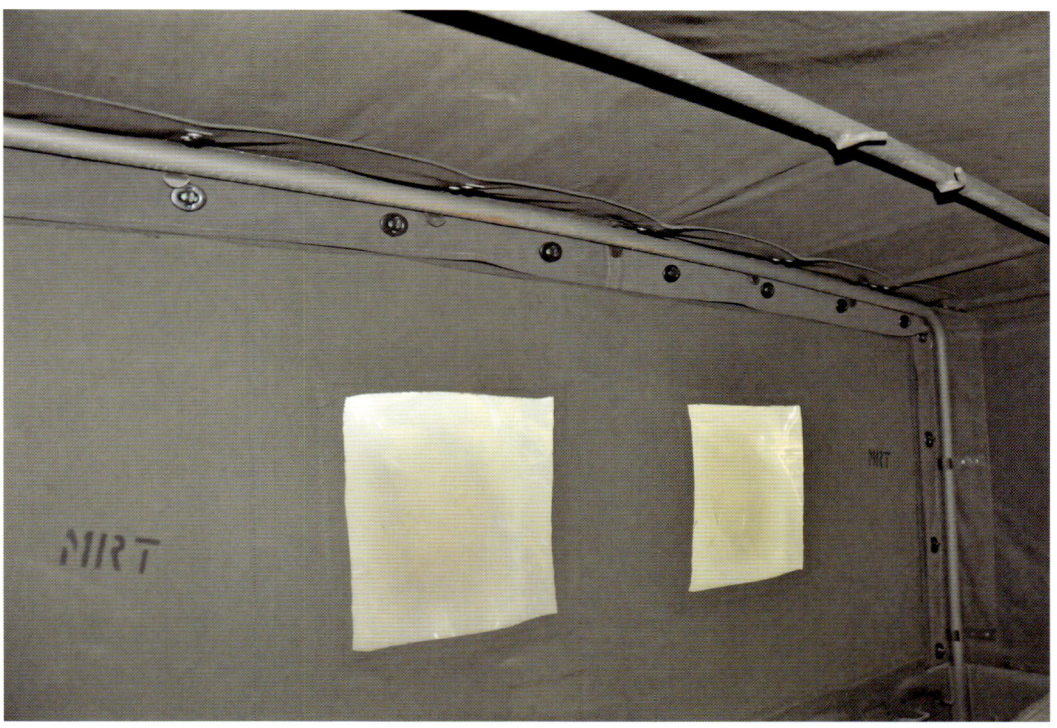

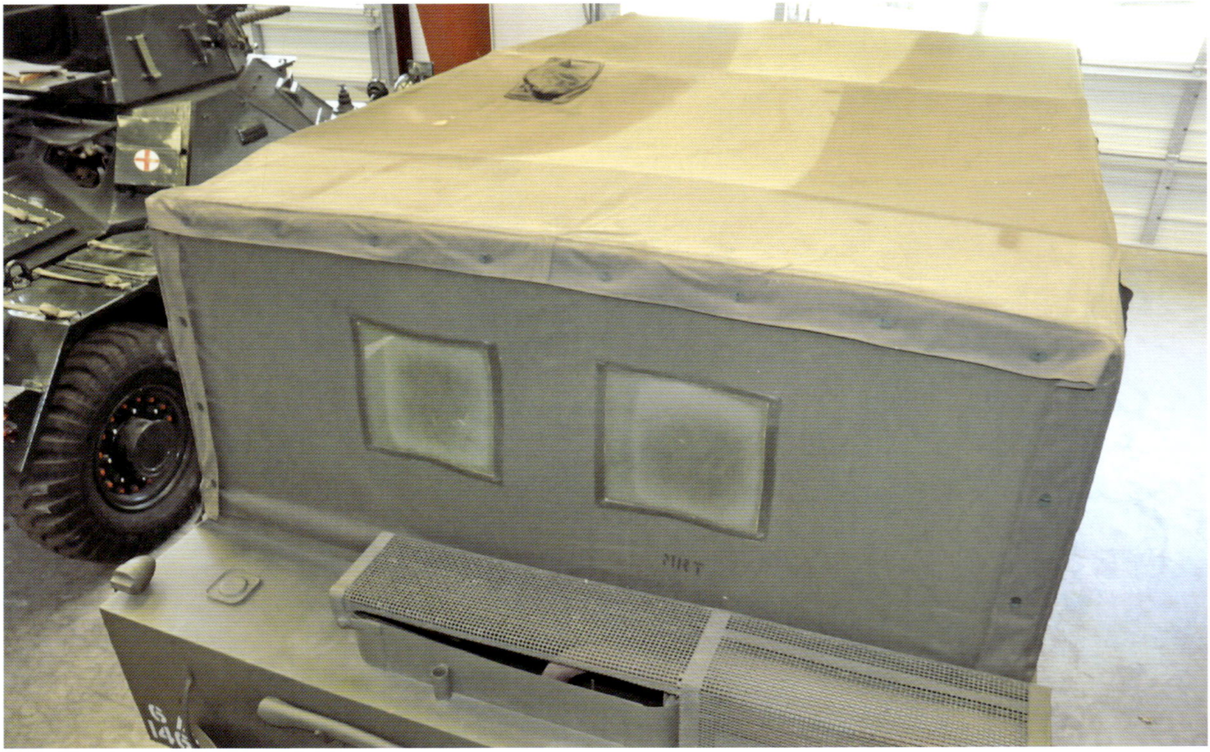

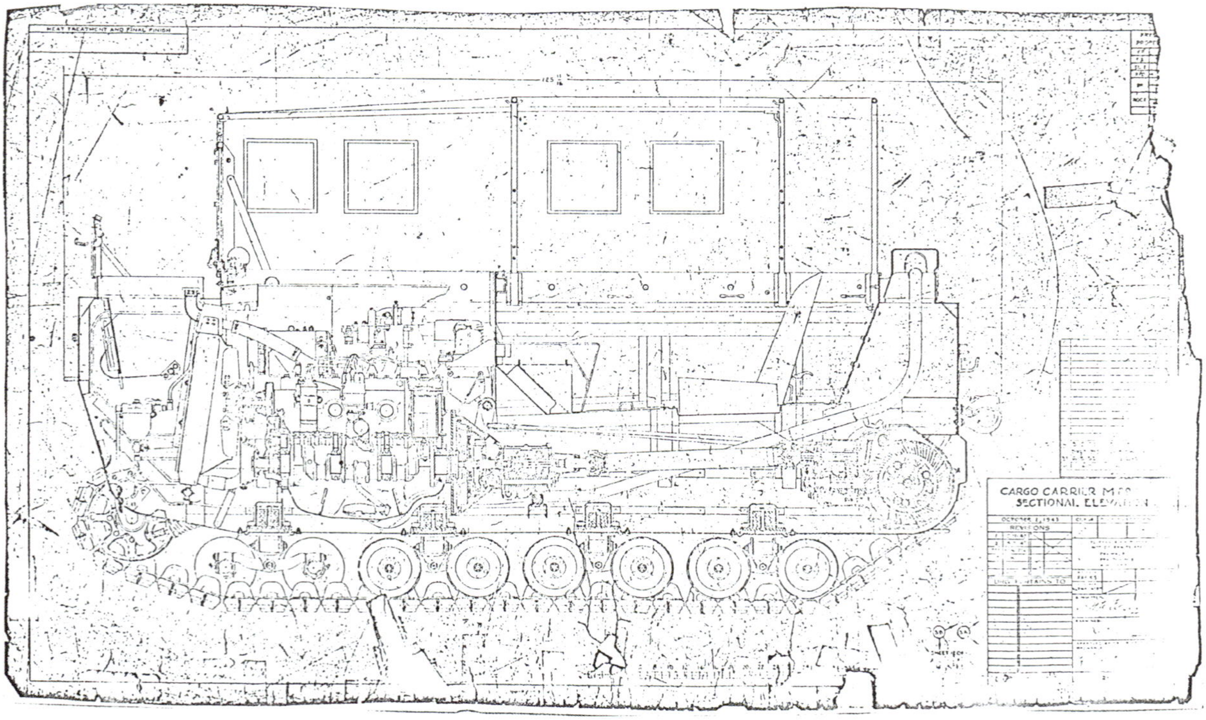
HEAT TREATMENT AND FINAL FINISH
CARGO CARRIER

Above: The canvas top and right side curtain of a Cargo Carrier M29 are viewed from above. The side curtain is in two pieces, with two plastic windows per panel. A splashguard runs along the side of the hull at the bottom of the sponson, and a step is at its midpoint. The canvas flap that was opened to erect a radio antenna above the vehicle is visible on the top. (Chris Hughes)

Opposite above: The canvas top and rear curtain are observed from the outside of the M29 cargo carrier. The dark feature on the left side of the top s a canvas flap to allow a radio antenna to protrude through the top. The outlines of the bows are visible on the top. (Chris Hughes)

Opposite below: In this cutaway drawing, the machinery layout of the M29 is plainly visible.

The right front of the canvas top is shown where it is attached to the right side of the windshield frame. A loop on the end of the cable that runs through the loops on the canvas top is secured to a pin below the hinge at the bottom of the windshield.

CHAPTER 3

The M29C

In April 1943 a standard T24 was tested in a lake, and performance was unsatisfactory. Speed was low and steering was non-responsive. Further tests showed that the tracks moved plenty of water – but unfortunately moved water in both directions, with the thrust from the returning tracks almost canceling that of the driving track.

To counter this and other problems, the vehicle was fitted with track skirts, a false bow and false stern. A discharge port was fashioned in the forward end of the track skirt, directing that water to the rear of the vehicle, forming in effect an auxiliary water jet assisting the lower track run.

The effect of all of this was to more than double the water speed of the vehicle. Freeboard was still markedly low, so it was decided that rather than a false bow and stern, flotation tanks should be installed in those areas. Various styles of rudder were tested, ultimately resulting in the decision being made to use two rudders mounted high on the stern flotation tank. The rudders, which swung freely on hinges to prevent damage from rocks and logs, could be lifted and stowed during land operation.

Ultimately the new vehicle, which NDRC personnel dubbed 'the Ark', was standardized as the M29C. The vehicle entered production at South Bend on 25 May 1944. Both the M29C and the M29 remained classified Standard A until July 1958, when they were reclassified as Standard B – a tribute to the superb engineering and production by the staffs of Studebaker and the NDRC.

Above: An assembly line worker guides an engine assembly into place in a Cargo Carrier M29C. As was the case with all Weasels, the M29C was powered by the Studebaker Model 6-170 six-cylinder, inline, L-head water-cooled engine, based on the Studebaker Champion engine. (National Archives)

Opposite above: Cargo Carrier M29C, Ordnance serial number 4913, appears in a 24 August 1944 photograph. Similar to the Cargo Carrier M29, the M29C had flotation cells in the front and the rear of the hull to improve the vehicle's performance while crossing water. (TACOM LCMC History Office)

Opposite below: The flotation cells of the M29C increased the overall length of the hull and gave it a more boat-like appearance. Unlike the M29, the M29C had rudders, shown here in the raised positions for operating on land. Track aprons also were installed below the sponsons. (TACOM LCMC History Office)

Cargo Carrier M29C, Ordnance serial number 4913, is viewed from above. On the coaming to the front of the driver's compartment is a tiller bar for controlling the rudders. The various control cables and linkages for the rudders are visible on the aft deck of the hull.

This overhead view of the driver's compartment shows the sparsely-padded seat, the instrument panel and, at far right, the open engine compartment.

The passenger's compartment of M29C, Ordnance number 4913, is viewed from the left. The passengers' seats were equipped with safety belts. To the front right of the compartment is a radio set. Stowed in the foreground is a boat hook.

A radio installation in an M29C is displayed. Several types of radios could be mounted in Weasels: principally, the SCR-506, -508, -510, -528, -608, -610, -628, -694, and -714. This set appears to be an SCR-610, a frequency-modulated, voice-operated model.

With the M29C, the Weasel family of tracked cargo carriers evolved from a vehicle designed for operation on snow, mud, or other difficult terrain, to a vehicle that was capable of all that plus operation on water. To achieve this transition to an amphibian vehicle, flotation cells were attached to the front and the rear of the hull, track skirting was added, and rudders were installed.

The surf guard on top of the bow flotation cell was designed to prevent the craft from shipping excess water. The surf guard pivoted on a pin on each side in order to swing it back over the deck to the front of the windshield for stowage for operation on land. Clamp-type latches on the rear of the surf guard served to hold it stationary.

The two hold-down latches for the surf guard are observed from another angle. The fitting bolted to the top of the flotation cell between the latches is a bull-nose chock. In the foreground is a hinged door allowing access to the interior of the bow cell.

The left hold-down latch of the surf guard is viewed from a distance, with the capstan in the center foreground. The latch features a T-handle with a coil spring inside; a hook on the front of the handle engages a U-shaped catch welded to the deck.

The bull-nose chock at the center front of the bow flotation cell is viewed from above. An eyebolt is mounted on the right side of the bull-nose. The bull-nose served to channel and direct the rope or line that was driven by the capstan on the bow flotation cell.

In the left background is the left pivot mounting for the surf guard. The rear of the guard is fastened with a pin to a bracket mounted on the deck. The pivot pin is secured in place with a nut and a cotter pin. The arrangement on the right side of the surf guard is similar.

As viewed from the left side of the bow, at the center is the capstan, used for pulling lines. Beyond the capstan are the blackout headlight and service headlight. The fuel filler cap is in the right background. In the right foreground is the capstan upper drive pulley.

Grouped on the right side of the bow flotation cell deck are, left to right, the service headlight and the blackout headlight. A brushguard for the headlights is welded to the deck. To the right is the capstan, powered by shafts from the engine crankshaft.

The service headlight is viewed close-up. This type of fixed headlight was introduced after serial number 3102, replacing the earlier type of removable spotlight that doubled as a headlight. The lighting system of the M29C was of a single-wire, grounded design.

The blackout headlight (left) and service headlight assemblies (right) are viewed from the rear. The electrical lines for these lights pass through holes in the lateral coaming to the lower left. This coaming marked the upper front edge of the M29-type hull.

To the right, fitted with a coaming around its perimeter, is the air duct for the radiator. At the front of the duct are the capstan drive belt and upper pulley. To the rear of the duct is the radiator filler cap. To the lower right, a 1-quart fire extinguisher is stowed on deck.

Fastened to a bracket on the deck to the front of the driver's compartment on the M29C is a fully adjustable rear-view mirror. Extending along the edge of the deck to the rear of the surf guard is a fixed coaming, fastened to the deck with hex screws and lock washers.

The fire extinguisher is viewed close-up from the centerline of the bow deck facing to the left. It is in a standard fire-extinguisher clamp-type holder. To the lower left, the Olive Drab interior of the coaming around the radiator air duct is in view.

The access door for the bow flotation cell is mounted on two hinges, with a door latch on the opposite side. This door provided access to cargo stowed within the cell and also provided a means of inspecting the cell for leakage, damage, and so on.

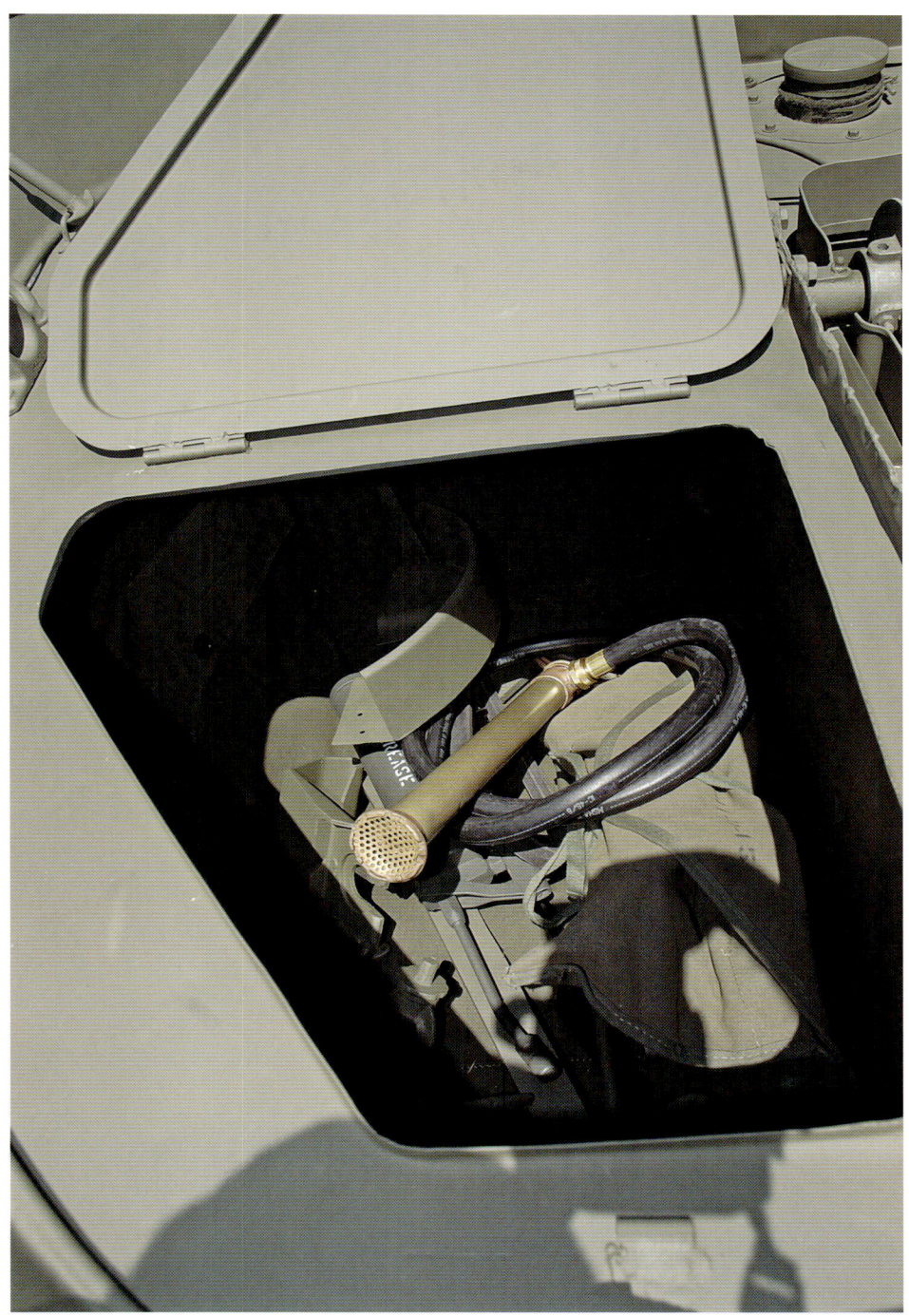

The bow flotation cell access door is open, as viewed from the left side of the bow. Among the gear stowed inside is a bilge pump. Each M29C was equipped with a portable, double-action bilge pump. The screen on the pump excluded foreign objects.

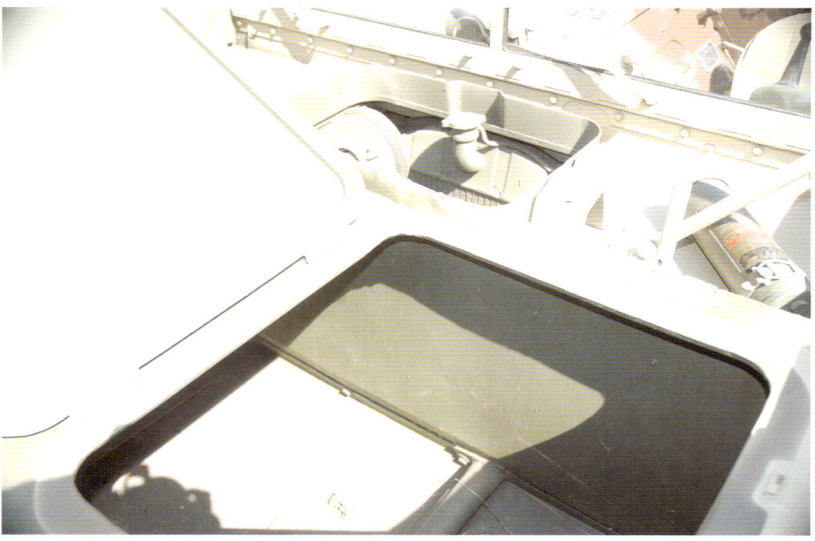

The open door to the interior of the bow flotation cell is observed from the left side of the vehicle. The two door hinges are of the butt-hinge type. In the right background are the radiator air duct, the radiator filler cap, the windshield, and windshield wipers.

In a view into the bow flotation cell from the front, barely discernible on the floor of the cell at the bottom center of the photo is a round inspection hole with a spring-hinged lid. The hole provides access to the bilge below the floor for pumping out bilge water.

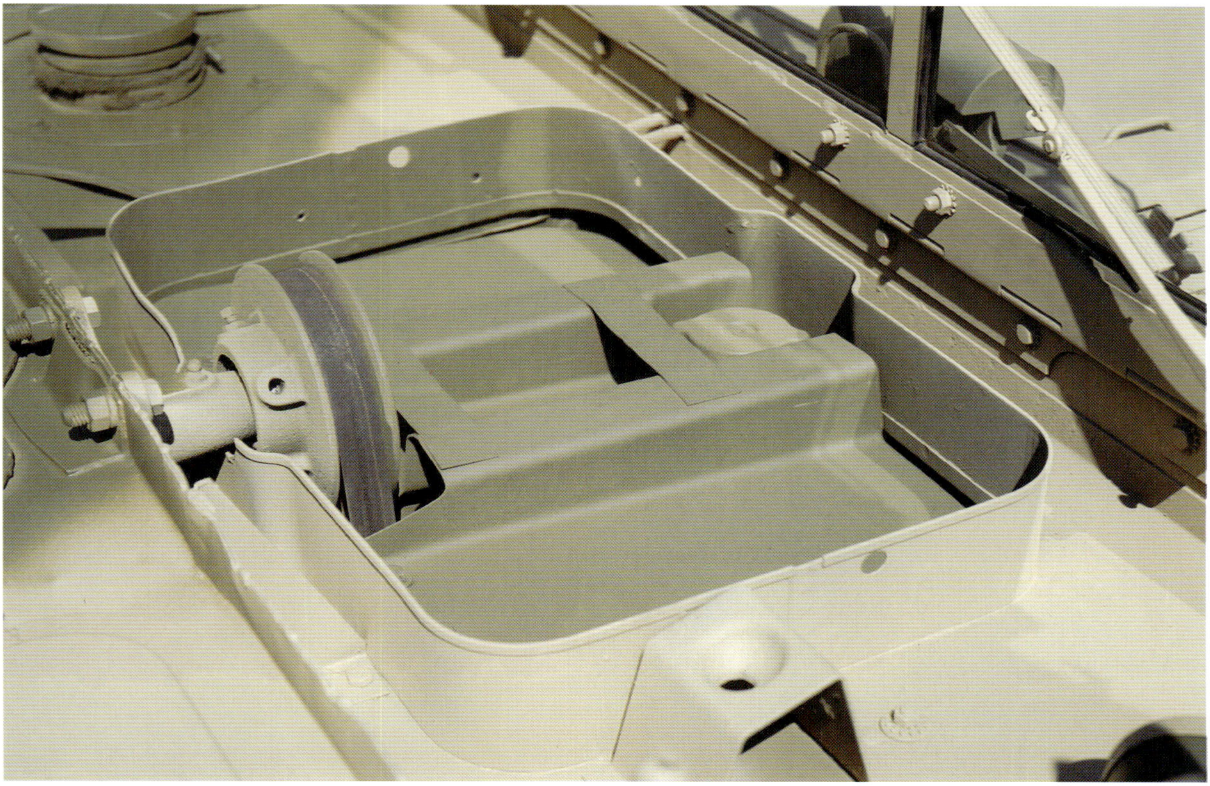

The radiator air duct is shown with the duct lid closed. The view is from the front left of the duct, with the windshield to the upper right.

In this view, the radiator air duct has been opened, allowing a clear view into the duct. To the rear of the duct are the radiator and the radiator filler cap. The tube running across the interior of the duct is the cross-shaft for operating the lid of the air duct.

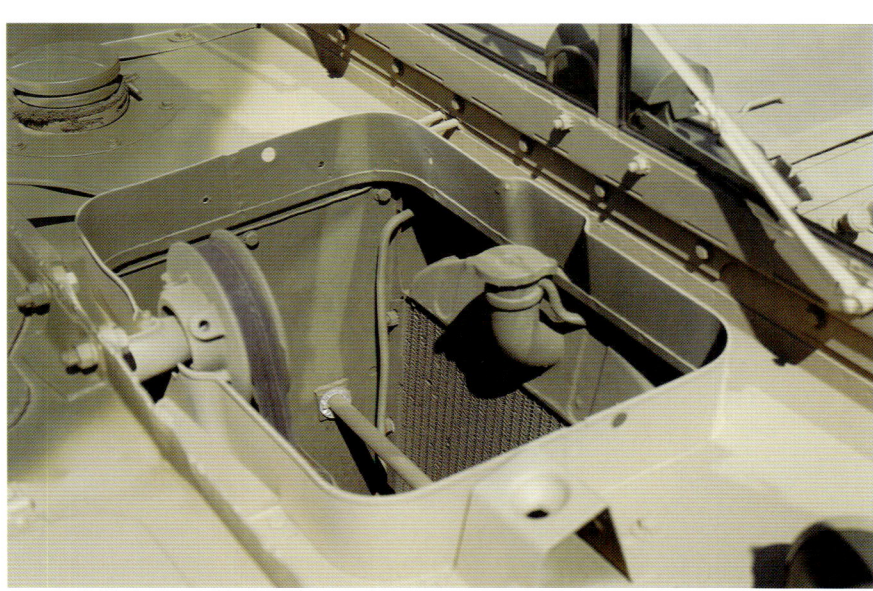

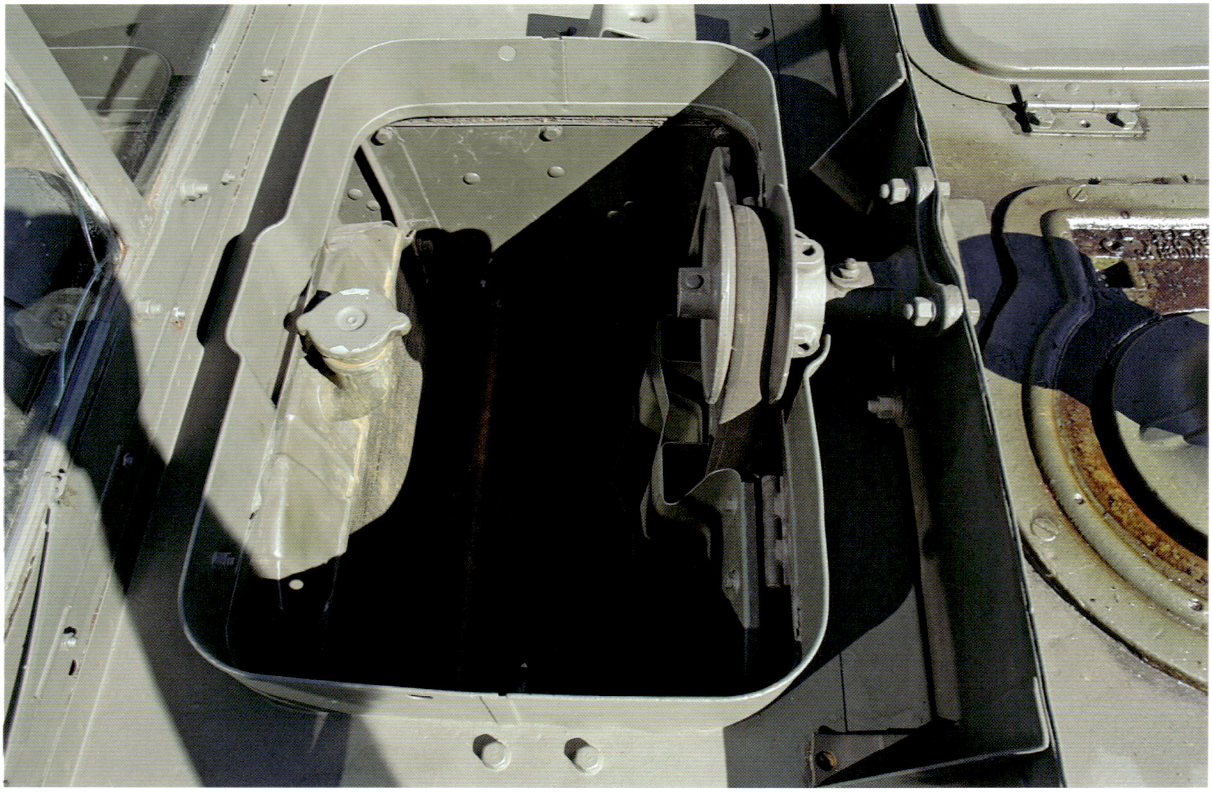

The lid of the radiator air duct is fully lowered in this view from the right of the duct. Incorporated into the design of the lid for the M29C were two channels, to provide clearance for the drive belt for the capstan when the lid was fully lowered.

The right side of the windshield is viewed from the front. The windshield assembly contains two glass panels in a steel frame that is hinged at the bottom so the assembly can be swung forward and lowered. The two electric windshield wipers are behind the glass.

The lower front of the bow flotation cell of an M29C is displayed. At the center is a horizontally oriented towing eye that was standard with M29Cs. To each side is a vertically oriented bracket that is not found on all vehicles. These are pivot mounts for a tow bar, a late production feature that was added to some earlier vehicles in accordance with a Modification Work Order.

The lower part of the bow flotation cell is shown from another angle, with the three towing eyes in view. The flotation cell was of welded and reinforced sheet-steel construction. A drain plug, not visible here, is included on the left bottom of the cell.

Above: A number of features are visible in this photograph taken from the left front of an M29C. In the foreground are the rear-view mirror and the radiator air duct. The entire windshield is shown, including the two windshield wipers driven by electric motors and, on the top left of the windshield, the manually operated wiper. To the rear of the windshield are the driver's seat, the engine compartment cover, and the instrument panel. To the rear are the passengers' seats.

Opposite above: A Cargo Carrier M29C is viewed from the left front. The surf guard is in the deployed position at the front of the bow flotation cell. The headlights are mounted high enough to shine over the guard. A brace is attached to the rear of each side of the windshield.

Opposite below: The left rear of the surf guard and the coaming to its rear are viewed. The stenciled instructions on the hull refer to drain plugs that were removed to let out bilge water. If the plugs were not reinserted before the vehicle entered the water, it could swamp.

INSTALL DRAIN PLUGS IN HULL BOTTOM
BEFORE ATTEMPTING TO FLOAT

Above: In the foreground is the left discharge orifice, above the front of the track. The orifice was designed in the form of a Pelton cup and channeled discharge water carried by the return, or upper, run of the tracks downward and to the rear, enhancing water performance.

Opposite above: The bow flotation cell was fastened to the hull with hex screws and washers. The aft edge of the flotation cell is slightly roughly cut, with many small burrs evident. A boat hook is stowed on the side of the hull, with this end of the handle resting in a U-shaped holder.

Opposite below: The hook end of the boat hook rests in a holder, and the hook is secured with a webbing strap through a footman loop on the deck. The two cables running alongside the coaming of the crew compartment are the control cables for the twin rudders.

Above: The discharge orifices had their origins in water tests of the M29 Weasel, where it was found that the force of water generated by the return tracks not only counteracted forward thrust, but also tended to swamp the vehicle. The discharge orifices fixed this problem.

Although not easily discernible, within the discharge orifices, inside the bottom of the bow flotation cell, are compound vanes. These vanes act to direct discharge water outboard and downward, reversing the natural direction of discharge water.

The left track skirting, or track apron, is displayed just aft of the discharge orifice. The skirting was mounted on hinges so it could be swung upward for performing maintenance on the tracks and suspension. One such hinge is visible in the foreground.

A Cargo Carrier M26C Weasel is observed from the left side, showing the canvas top and rear curtain in place over the driver's and passengers' compartments. The flotation cells added almost five feet to the overall length of the M29C as compared to the M29: the M29 had an overall hull length of 9 feet 11 inches exclusive of the pintle hook, while the M29C had an overall hull length of 14 feet $4\frac{19}{32}$ inches.

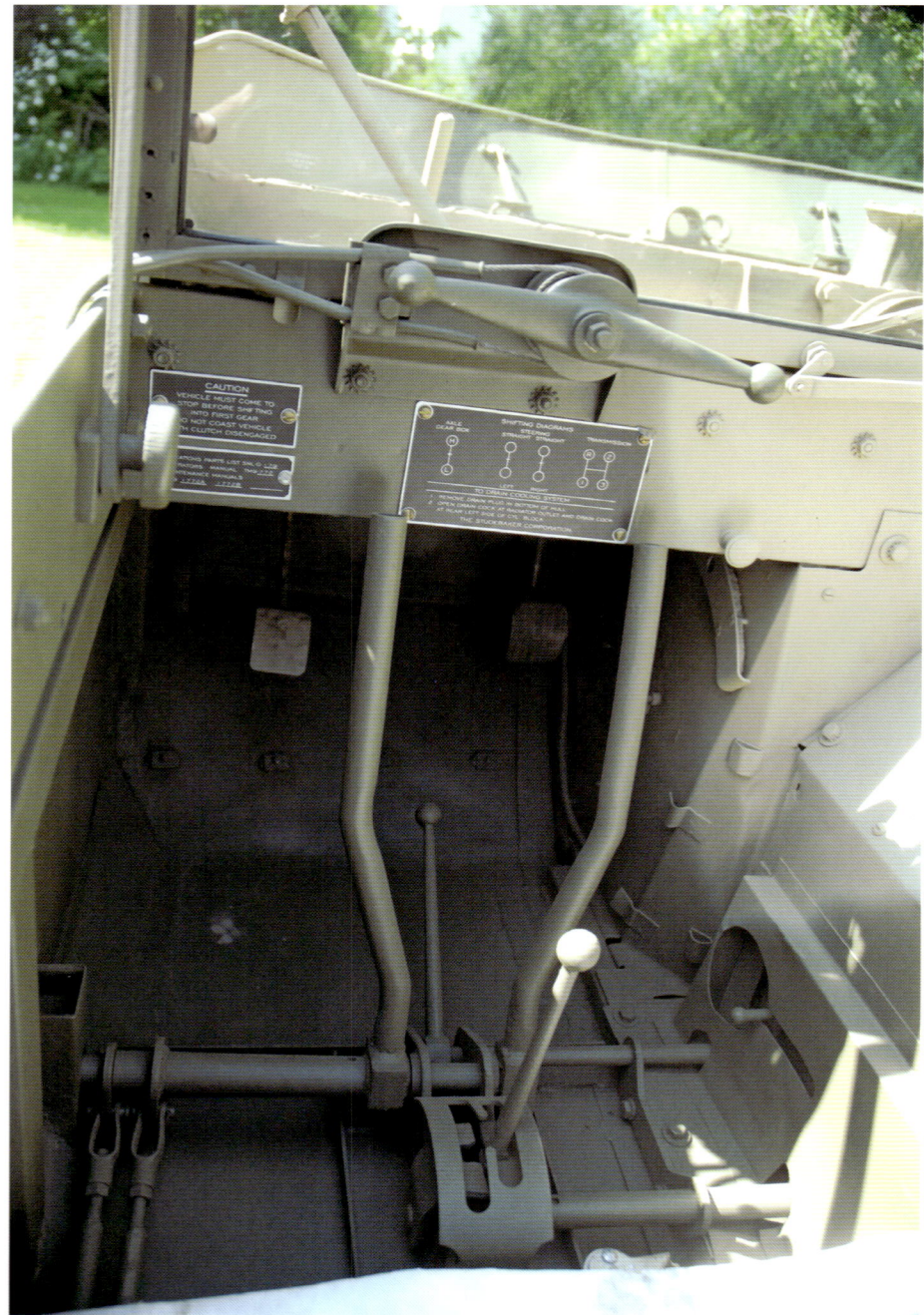

The layout of the driver's controls in the M29C is similar to that of the M29, except that on the coaming of the M29C is a tiller, by means of which the driver controlled the rudders during operation on water. Mounted on the floor are the steering levers, between and to the front of which is the axle-gearbox shift lever. To the rear of the steering levers is the transmission lever, with three forward gears and reverse.

The tiller is visible from the side through the space between the left side of the windshield and the slanting brace to the rear of the windshield. Steel cables are wrapped around the shaft of the tiller, and these control cables passed through the guide tube in the lower foreground and back to the rudders. In the background, part of the instrument panel and the electric windshield motors are visible.

Above: The tiller has ball-shaped grips on the ends. Turning the tiller clockwise steers the vehicle to the right during water operation, and turning it counter-clockwise steers the vehicle to the left. To the right of the tiller is the operating arm for the left windshield wiper.

Opposite above: Instructional and cautionary placards are affixed to the coaming at the front of the driver's compartment. The one to the right includes shifting instructions and directions on draining the cooling system. Toward the left is a knob securing the windshield brace.

Opposite below: The gauges on the instrument panel are, left to right: fuel gauge, oil-pressure gauge, voltmeter, ammeter, engine-heat indicator, and speedometer. To the upper right of the panel is the primer knob. To the upper left of the panel is the engine starter switch.

Above: Aft of the instrument panel is a small engine access door, to the rear of which is the master electrical switch. The fitting attached to the top of the engine-compartment cover is a foot pocket to hold a stretcher. In the keyhole-shaped opening at the lower left is the heat-outlet control.

Opposite above: Details of the right side of the rear of the windshield are observed. The two electric motors at the bottom of the windshield frame actuate the operating arms connected to the windshield wipers. A switch is visible on the near end of each motor housing.

Opposite below: The electric motors for the windshield wipers are viewed from the right side of an M29C. The electrical cables are plugged into sockets on the sill below the motors. In the foreground, the cover of the engine compartment has been removed.

The left windshield-wiper motor is shown. The power cord has been unplugged from the socket on the sill to the right of the motor. The button-shaped object on the sill toward the lower right is the fuel-valve control for regulating the flow of fuel to the heater.

The cover of the engine compartment of an M29 is standing on end. The view is facing the inside of the cover. To the right is the inboard edge of the cover; the screws and nuts on that side of the cover are for securing a maintenance placard and stretcher foot pocket.

The M29C's driver's seat has a cushioned bottom and back. The sides of the seat back curve forward to cradle the driver's back. The two pedals to the front of the steering levers are: left, the clutch pedal, and right, the accelerator pedal. Braking was achieved by pulling back on both steering levers. In either forward or reverse gears, pulling back on the right steering lever steered the vehicle to the right, and pulling the left lever steered it to the left. (Rick Forys)

Above: On the stretcher foot pocket atop the engine-compartment cover, the L-shaped pin that locked the stretcher foot in place when the M29C was carrying litter patients is secured to the pocket with a retainer chain. The placard contains a daily maintenance schedule.

Opposite above: Faintly visible to the right of the right steering lever is the handle for operating the radiator air-duct lid. On the coaming to the right of the top of the right steering lever is the throttle control. To the far right are placards for maximum speed and vehicle data.

Opposite below: The engine-compartment enclosure is shown with the cover removed. Two catches with wing nuts below the inboard top edge of the enclosure serve to lock the cover in place when installed. Toward the right above the data plates is the master electrical switch.

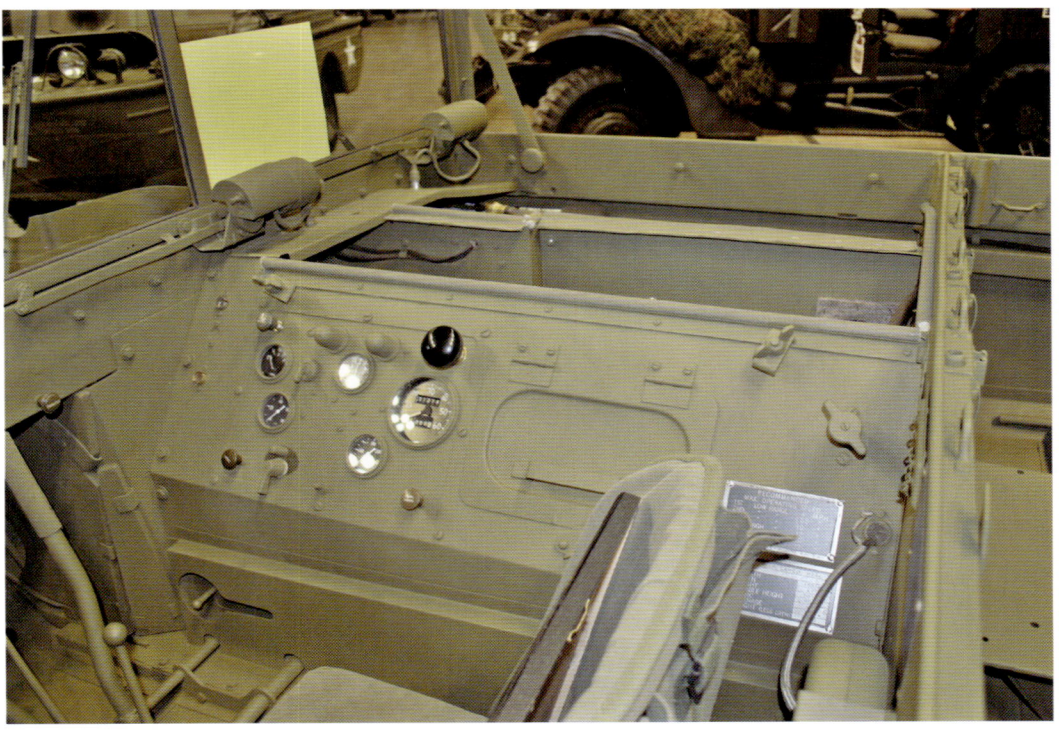

In the passenger compartment, the floor pan is removable to provide access to mechanisms in the lower hull. The rack at the center held optional demolition equipment. On the floor to the right rear of the shelf is the transmission inspection cover.

Three passengers' seats are in the M29C. The seat cushions are removable and are held in place by a hold-down strap at the front and at the back of the cushion. The seat backs are also removable by unhooking the lower rear of the back, tipping it forward, and pulling it.

Stowed in the left rear corner of the passenger compartment is a spotlight. The rear of the spotlight housing is at the top. On the corner of the coaming above the spotlight is a bow pocket, for inserting the rear bow, one of several that support the canvas top and curtains. At the top are the rear blackout marker lamp and a stretcher foot pocket.

The rear deck and the rear of the passenger compartment of an M29C are observed from the left side. To the rear of the passenger compartment is the muffler guard, and straddling the guard is a bracket supporting a radio antenna and mast base.

The front left part of the passenger compartment of an M29C. Two transverse channel sections increase the strength of the forward bulkhead of the compartment. The Olive Drab devices with coil springs hanging from the channel are stretcher hangers.

At the center front of the passenger compartment is a rack for demolition equipment. In operations where demolition equipment was authorized, the top of the shelf held a power pack and a demolition-bomb case. The equipment also included a detonator and a timer.

Above: Affixed to the inside of the sill running around the passengers' compartment is a nomenclature plate that reads 'M-29-C-7195,' the number 7195 being the manufacturer's hull number.

Below: This cross section view of a M29C clearly shows the density of the mechanical components within the vehicle.

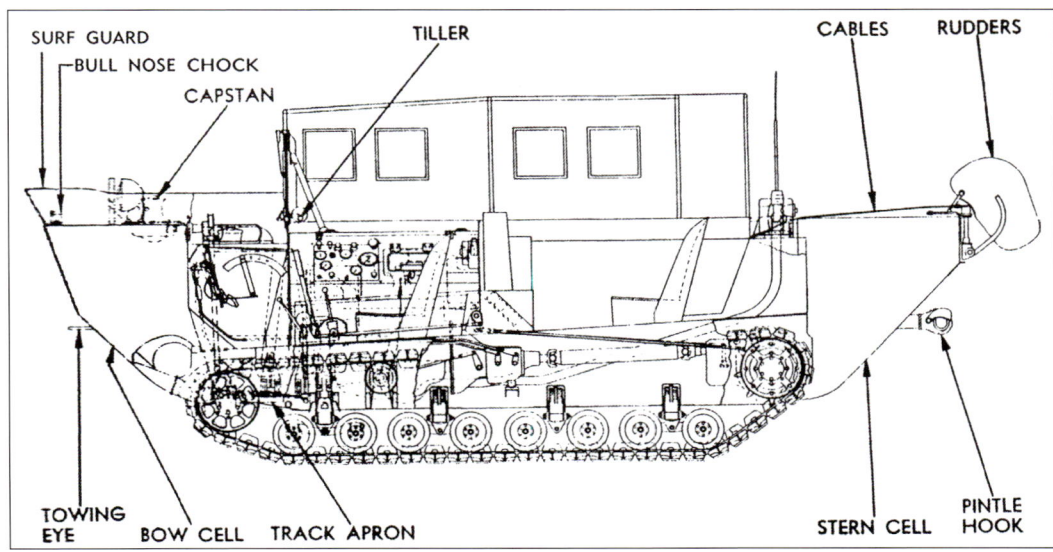

The rudders, which were on pivoting mounts so they could be folded up and out of the way for operation on land, are deployed in the lowered position for operating on water in this view of an M29C. Between the rudders, on the center of the vertical rear plate of the stern flotation cell, is an electrical socket and sprung lid for powering the lights of a towed vehicle. This socket was a modification the Norwegians performed on their M29Cs post-war.

The rudders are pivoted up and secured. A clamp-type holder fastened to both rear corners of the flotation cell deck is hooked through a hole in the corresponding rudder to hold it in place. The rudders are welded to the curved, lower portions of the rudder posts.

A rear-facing blackout marker lamp is on the left front corner of the stern flotation cell. Next to it is a stretcher foot pocket. Guide tubes for the rudders are also in the foreground. In the background are stowed pioneer tools: a shovel and an axe.

The blackout marker lamp and a stretcher foot pocket are displayed. Stretchers typically had 'feet,' or small legs, made of bent metal strapping. The foot pockets served to secure the feet of the stretchers in place by means of L-shaped pins inserted through the sides.

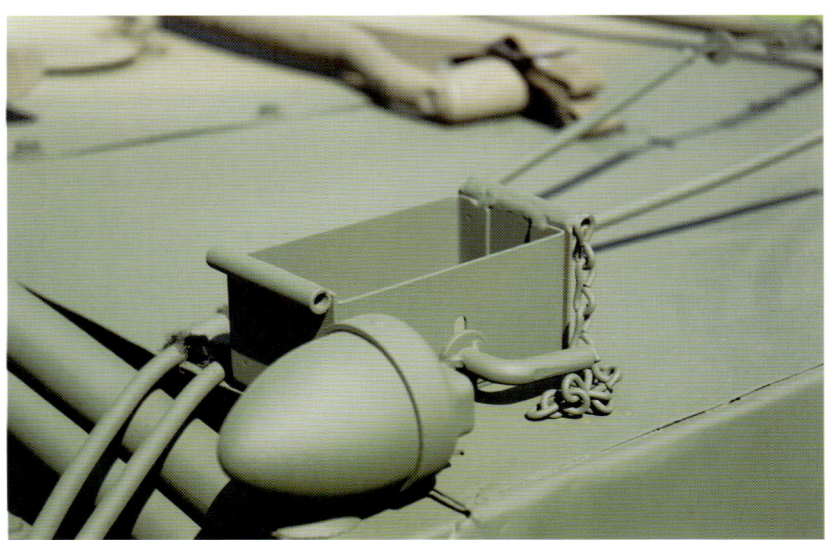

The disk-shaped object between the axe and the shovel atop the stern flotation cell is an inspection door, fitted with a sprung hinge. This provided a means of inspecting the cell for leaks and damage and for inserting a bilge pump to clear the cell of water.

The rear ends of the rudder cables are attached with adjustable clevises to each side of the operating arm attached to the top of the left rudder post. A tie rod called the cross shaft transmits movement of the left rudder to the operating arm of the right rudder.

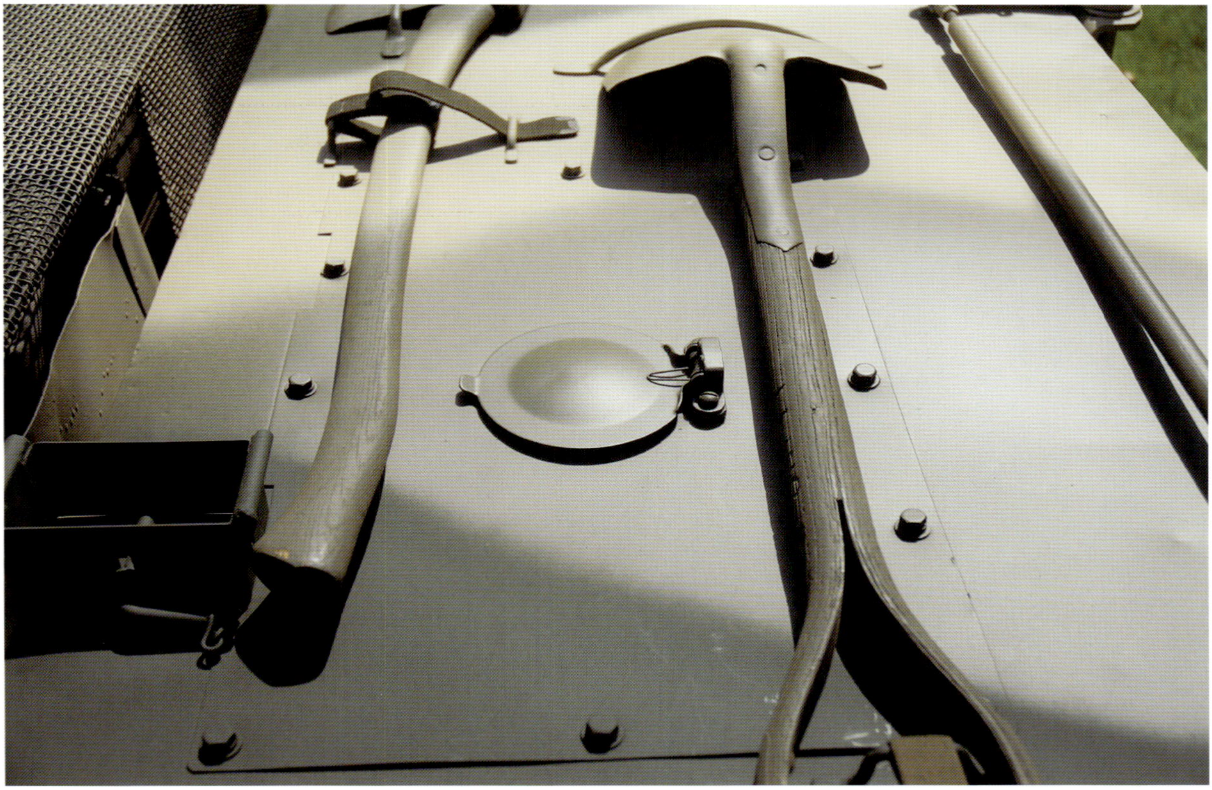

Below the pioneer tools on the deck of the stern flotation cell is a removable sheet-steel lid, secured with hex screws, for gaining access to the interior of the cell if necessary. At the center of the plate are the flotation cell inspection door and its sprung hinge.

The raised rudders are viewed from the left rear of the M29C, showing how they are secured by means of clamp-type holders. Both sides of the left rudder's operating arm are visible from this angle; it forms a T-shape above the top of the rudder post.

The right rudder is displayed, along with its operating arm. The right side of the cross shaft is attached to the rudder operating arm by means of a clevis. When the rudder cables moved the left rudder, the cross shaft translated that movement to the right rudder.

In a view of an M29C from the rear, the rudder mechanisms are visible. The upper parts of the rudder posts are positioned in brackets bolted to the rear horizontal plate of the stern flotation cell. Just below the rudder brackets are the yokes that allow for the pivoting of the rudders for travel on land. A hinge pin secures the top of the curved part of the rudder post – that is, the part of the post welded to the rudder – to the yoke. The electrical receptacle between the rudder posts is a post-war Norwegian modification.

On the deck of the stern flotation cell are stowed a shovel and an axe. To the front of that deck are the muffler guard and exhaust lines. Further forward are the passengers' and driver's compartments and the windshield, with the headlights in the right distance.

A pintle hook is attached to the lower plate at the rear of the stern flotation cell for towing operations. Early-production Weasels had a swivel-style pintle hook, while late-production examples had a fixed pintle hook, as seen in this photograph.

The stationary pintle hook on a Cargo Carrier M29C is fastened to its bracket with four large hex screws. Welded seams on the sheet-steel skin of the stern flotation cell are visible, including a horizontal one in line with the center of the pintle hook.

The yoke where the lower part of the right rudder post pivots on the upper part of the rudder post is displayed, with the rudder in the raised position. The yoke, and consequently the rudder, moves in unison with the upper part of the rudder post.

The rudder of this M29C, secured in the 'up' position by the clamp-type holder, is welded rather roughly to the lower, curved part of the rudder post. Various weld patterns are observed on different M29C rudders, including three neatly executed tack welds.

The hole in the rudder of an M29C for attaching the hook of a clamp-type holder is apparent. The sheet metal of the side of the hull wraps around the upper plate of the stern and is welded, the weld being visible about an inch from the corner of the hull.

Details of the right rudder post, bracket, and rudder arm of a Cargo Carrier M29C are displayed. The clamp holder for securing the rudder in the 'up' position for travel on land is on a pivoting mount attached to the rudder arm above the center of the photograph.

The left rudder is in the raised position for travel on land, with the clamp holder attached to it, while the right rudder is in the lowered position, as it would be deployed for operating in the water. The rudder posts are welded to the left side of each rudder.

A Cargo Carrier M29C is observed from the right rear. During the development of the M29C, various designs and combinations of rudders were experimented with. The best steering response was achieved with twin rudders, mounted as high on the stern flotation cell as possible. The yokes incorporated into the rudder posts allowed the rudders to swing freely, which often prevented damage to them from striking rocks, logs, and other objects in the water.

The M29C could achieve a speed in water of four miles per hour. By contrast, it was capable of a speed on land of 36mph. The shape of the stern flotation cell and the position of the bottom of its sponsons on a tangent with the return tracks helped divert part of the slipstream away from the return-track chambers.

Above: The rear of the right track skirting is displayed. This section of skirting has two hinges on its upper edges. Removing the cotter pins in these catches frees the skirt section to be removed to allow access to the tracks, the idler wheel, and other components.

Opposite above: The rear section of the right track skirting is shown from another angle, displaying more details of the two hinges. The track skirting was essential to the optimal performance of the M29C in water, and removing the skirting would degrade that performance.

Opposite below: The deck atop the stern flotation cell of an M29C is observed from the right side. Simple, bow-shaped brackets, welded to the deck, were provided for securing the shovel and the axe. Webbing straps attached to footman loops completed the securing of these tools.

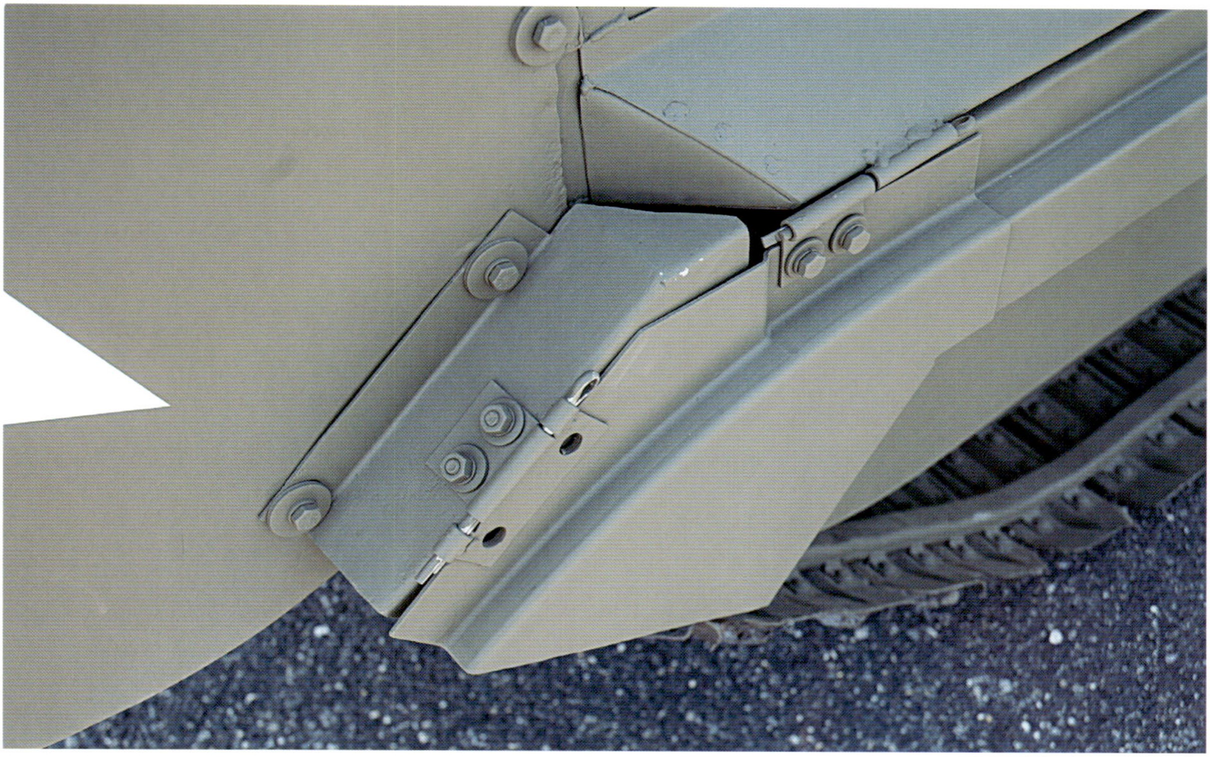

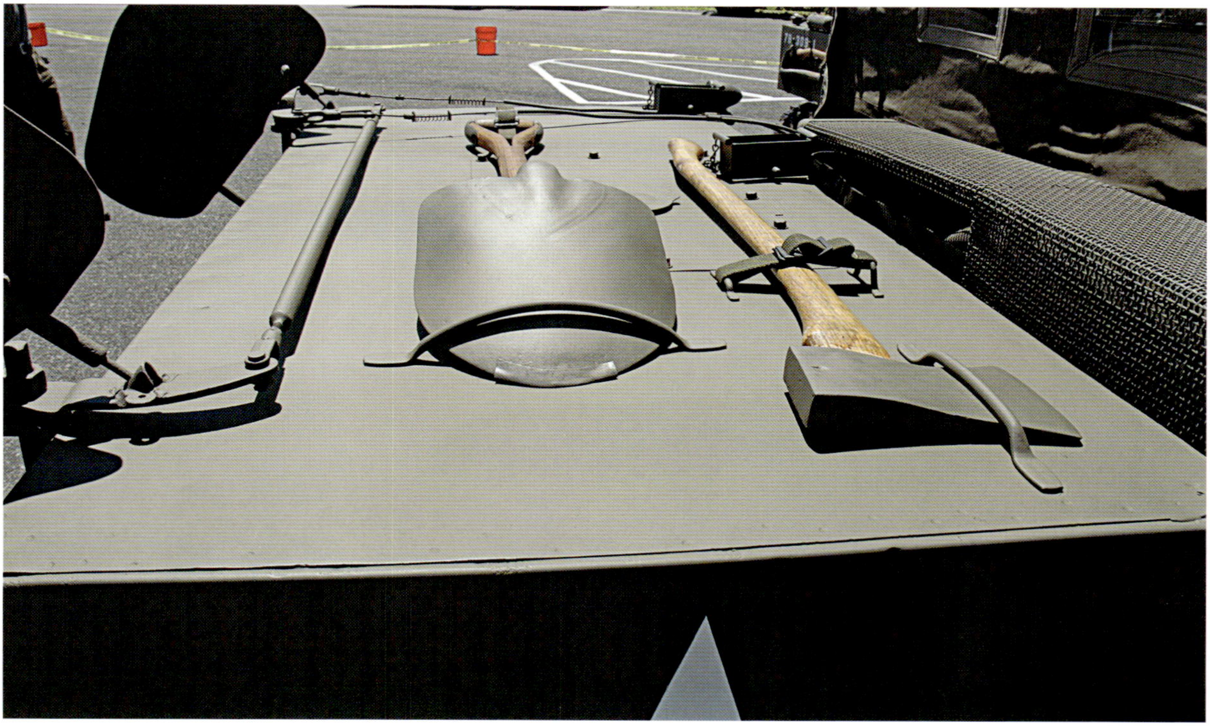

The muffler is mounted between the rear of the passenger compartment and the stern flotation cell deck. The muffler is oblong in section and is oriented vertically. Surrounding the sides and the top of the muffler is the steel-mesh muffler guard.

This M29C on display at the US Army Transportation Museum is fitted with a canvas top – probably an improvised top from a cargo truck – with a large, rectangular plastic window on the rear curtain instead of the commonly seen configuration of two square plastic windows in the rear of the curtain.

On each side of the M29C, hidden behind the track skirting, are two tubular, horizontal braces for the skirting. To lift or remove the skirting for vehicle maintenance, two hook-type fasteners, such as this one, are released, freeing the braces from the skirting.

A simple, spring steel rod forms the hook, which engages a hole in the brace, trapping the hinged track skirt in the down position.

The top of the track skirting of the M29C is just above the series of holes. Above the skirting is an angled fender, a change in the hull design required when the 20-inch tracks were introduced with the M29C as opposed to the 15-inch track used by the M29/T24.

The forward right part of an M29C's track skirting is shown. On restored M29Cs, several designs of tracks are observed. On this one, a continuous rubber belt, attached to the track shoes with tabs, is to each side of the standard rubber belts astride the center of the track.

The track skirting on the right side of an M29C is viewed facing to the rear. The forward skirting-brace fastener is visible about midway down the skirting, and the rear fastener is present further aft. The outer rubber belt and mounting tabs on the track are visible.

The discharge orifice on the right side of an M29C is shown. To raise or remove the track skirting for maintenance on the tracks or suspension, it was necessary to remove the cotter pin at the bottom of the discharge orifice and another pin at the rear of the skirting.

Above: The right discharge orifice at the bottom right of the bow flotation cell of an M29C is viewed from above and to the rear. The forward horizontal hinge of the track skirting is on the ledge to the rear of the orifice and is secured with a large cotter pin.

Opposite above: Tools carried on an M29C included some generic ones and some specialized ones. At the center are elements of a suspension lifter. Toward the lower right are a jack and a jack crank. Also present are a rope, hammer, screwdriver, pliers, and various wrenches.

Opposite below: Additional tools for an M29C are displayed. To the upper right is an essential piece of equipment for this amphibian vehicle: a hand-operated bilge pump. The second tool to the right at the upper left of the photo is an idler-wheel tension-spring release bracket.

David Welch, who restored the M29C depicted here, connects the elements of a suspension lifter to the vehicle. His left hand is on a screw jack attached to a special bracket that is hooked over the coaming. His right hand is holding the top of a link that will be attached to the jack at the top and to the suspension yoke at the bottom. The jack and link pull the suspension up.

With its bow flotation cell, and with the surf plate deployed in the forward position, the M29C presented a very boatlike appearance from the front, entirely unlike the boxy, snub-nosed appearance of the model's predecessors from the T15 to the M29. As can be seen from this photograph, when the surf plate is deployed it somewhat limits the driver's forward field of vision.

A Cargo Carrier M29C comes ashore. The sheet metal of the bow flotation cell shows evidence of battering over the years. A rope boat fender is draped over the front of the cell to protect it from bumps. The tops of the bows are visible above the hull.

In a right front view of the restored M29C, the sheet metal of the bow has suffered battering over the decades, leaving numerous dents on the surface. Also, the side panels of the hull are not perfectly flat and smooth, exhibiting signs of occasional battering. A small amount of corrosion is visible on the tracks.

Above: US soldiers in an M29, registration number 40152034, are herding a group of German prisoners of war captured near Saint-Jean-de-Daye, Normandy, down a road toward Saint-Lô on 11 July 1944. Note the guard to the front of the radiator air duct, and the two steps on the splashguard. (National Archives)

Opposite above: Troopers of the First Special Service Force prepare to use a T24 to move medical supplies and food over the Rapido River in Italy. The supplies are being taken to the beleaguered 143rd Infantry on 23 January 1944. The 143rd suffered more casualties during this action than any other during the unit's history. (National Archives)

Opposite below: A Cargo Carrier M29 of the 993rd Engineer Treadway Bridge Company crosses the River Seine near Mautes, France, on a steel treadway bridge on 22 August 1944. With the gap between the tracks too narrow to fit on both treadways, one track is riding on the beam of one of the treadways. A rolled tarpaulin and other equipment are piled high on the engine compartment behind the right side of the windshield. (National Archives)

Warrant Officer William Thomas of Burlington, Vermont, a maintenance officer in the 85th Division, drives a Cargo Carrier T24, registration number 401217823, on a mountain road in the Quinzano area of Italy on 21 October 1944. On the hull to the front and the rear of the identification star are unusual fittings, purpose not known. Also, two triangular fittings with holes through them are on each side of the coaming; one of them is adjacent to Thomas. (National Archives)

In the fall of 1944, the M29s, which were designed for operating on snow, proved themselves very useful on the muddy roads and fields of northwestern Europe. Here, an M29 is being used as a carrier on muddy, rutted ground at an ordnance field depot in France on 4 November 1944. (National Archives)

Above: Members of a B-26 medium-bomber crew of the 497th Bomb Squadron, 344th Bomb Group, Ninth Air Force, pile into an M29 Weasel at Schoppen, Belgium, on 23 January 1944. These airmen had been touring the front lines to familiarize themselves with the operations of ground forces in that sector, and they were about to return to their base. The vehicle has been whitewashed to blend in with the snowy terrain. (National Archives)

Opposite above: M29Cs were making their way to the European Theater by late 1944. This example, assigned to Ninth US Army Headquarters in France, is shown negotiating a 35-degree slope on 8 November 1944. The railroad-style registration number painted in white to the front of the windshield is P5853207. The front and rear flotation chambers bolted to the hull gave the M29C an amphibious capability; the vehicle was therefore dubbed the 'Water Weasel'. (National Archives)

Opposite below: Featuring a winter-camouflage paint scheme reminiscent of a Dalmatian dog's coat, an M29 carries wounded GIs of the 3rd Battalion, 16th Infantry Regiment, 1st Infantry Division, to an aid station near Weywertz, Belgium, on 15 January 1945. Two litters bearing patients are laid laterally on top of the coaming. A fabric cover with matching camouflage and two small vision flaps is fitted over the windshield. (National Archives)

Above: The railroad-type registration number on the hull of this M29C, about to take to the water in Washington, DC, on 24 January 1945, reads 40184217. 'HQ-12' is marked in white on the bow. The headlight and brush guard are visible on the right side of the front deck. Note the large dent on the bow of the front flotation chamber. (National Archives)

Opposite above: Two wounded GIs of the 18th Infantry Regiment, 1st Infantry Division, wounded during the taking of Hepschied, Belgium, are being evacuated on an M29 Weasel to an aid station on 28 January 1945. This vehicle was US Army registration number 40152226-S, one of 1,000 M29s constructed under contract W-271-ORD-7197. Note the dark-colored identification star and the marking 'POOL' on the left front of the vehicle. (National Archives)

Opposite below: Medics on an M29 work to get a litter patient comfortable prior to evacuating him to an aid station somewhere in the European theater of operations on 30 January 1945. These medics were attached to the 78th Infantry Division, Ninth US Army. Stenciled on the side of the hull of the M29 is 'PREPARED BY L.T.D. / May 9, 1944.' (National Archives)

Above: A large assemblage of M29C Weasels parked in a yard at the 851st Ordnance Depot at München Gladbach, Germany, on 15 March 1945. The first two vehicles on the right have signs painted on the hulls that appear to read 'PROCESSED BY' followed by an illegible name and the date, month ['MAR'] and year [(19)45]. Those first two M29Cs have their surf guards in the raised position. The first vehicle is USA number 40185844-S. (National Archives)

Opposite above: An M29 Weasel is being employed in evacuating a wounded trooper of the 82nd Airborne Division during the drive on Herresbach, Belgium, on 29 January 1945. The registration number on the hull is 40176866. In this case, the litter is arranged fore-to-aft on the left side of the cargo compartment. (National Archives)

Opposite below: A driver is putting an M29C Water Weasel through its paces during a familiarization demonstration in the moat of picturesque Hoensbroek Castle, Holland, on 14 March 1945. Personnel from the 30th and the 79th Divisions, Ninth US Army, were taking turns driving the vehicle on land and water, to get an idea of its performance and capabilities. Note the side panels of the canvas top on the right side; the driver has folded his left-side panel up onto the roof. (National Archives)

Above: Infantrymen of the 383rd Battalion, 96th Division, receive a resupply of water and rations from three M29C Weasels on Okinawa on 2 April 1945. Marked on the upper left quarter of the bows of the Weasels is '3 HQ' and the order of march; '12' on the first vehicle. What appears to be a small emblem or insignia is on the upper center of each bow: a shield with a cross on it. (National Archives)

Opposite above: Vehicles, including two M29C Weasels in the foreground, are part of a traffic tie-up due to a muddy road ahead on Okinawa on 24 May 1945. In addition to the 'US ARMY' stencils on the Weasels, the only other visible markings are '2HQ-4' on the left vehicle and '2HQ-3' on the one to the right. A wooden crate for demolition blocks is on the rear of the Weasel to the right. (National Archives)

Opposite below: Members of a US Army Signal Corps unit are using an M29C while rigging a telephone line through a rice paddy, between Sukiran and Koza, Okinawa, on 15 June 1945. The vehicle is almost totally covered in mud. Weasels performed exceptionally well in muddy, marshy, and swampy terrain, including rice paddies. (National Archives)

Above: During the late-summer rainy season in Korea, Weasels were often called upon to transport men, ammunition, and rations to the front lines. This M29C, USMC registration number 114093, is hauling several members of the 1st Marine Division down a steep, muddy road east of Chang-dan on 29 August 1952. The driver was Sgt. Lynn N. Huckabay. (National Archives)

Opposite above: Two wounded GIs have been loaded onto M29 registration number 40151975-S of the 30th US Division at a medical evacuation point near Bruckhauser, Germany, on 25 March 1945. What appears to be a *gendarmeriehelm* (police helmet) is strapped to the grille on the front deck. A hand-operated horn is on the left side of the windshield frame. (National Archives)

Opposite below: Viewed from the left rear in a 1947 photograph, this M29C, registration number 40197787, at Fort Lewis, Washington, in 1947, was equipped for work as an ambulance. For winterization purposes, the vehicle had a hardtop made of plywood on a wooden frame, with a folding rear panel with a window in the center. The interior of the enclosure is unpainted. (National Archives)

Above: Members of B Company, 51st Signal Battalion, pull S-4 communications cable from a reel on an M29C Weasel assigned to A Company, 51st Signal Battalion, in Korea on 16 August 1954. The crew was running communications lines across this river. Long rods were inserted through the six reels of cable on the M29C, and the rods were resting in notches cut in the wooden rack. The registration number is visible on the hull: 40196785.(National Archives)

Opposite above: The same mud-spattered Marine M29C seen in the photo on page 139, registration number 114093, is proceeding on its way east of Chang-dan on 29 August 1952. In addition to being marked on the bow, 'USMC 114093' is also painted at the center of the side of the hull, directly below the face of the Marine sitting in the rear of the vehicle. (National Archives)

Opposite below: Members of A Company, 51st Signal Battalion, I US Corps, lay S-4 communications cable from an M29C Weasel at a river crossing in Korea on 16 August 1954. On the M29 is a locally built wooden rack that holds six reels of cable. On the body of the vehicle to the front of the identification star is a stencil warning to install drain plugs in the hull before attempting to operate on water. (National Archives)

Above: An M29 assigned to Company C, 1st Battalion, 12th Infantry Regiment, is breaking a trail while transporting heavy equipment during Exercise Little Bear, north of Anchorage, Alaska, on 9 February 1960. The Weasel has a tall enclosure on it, with snowshoes stored on the roof. The vehicle is towing what the original caption of the image describes as an 'oakie,' which is a trailer with stakes, mounted on what appears to be tracks. (National Archives)

Opposite above: M29C Weasel registration number 40196785 of A Company, 51st Signal Battalion, is being employed in stringing S-4 communications cables across irrigation ditches at a site in Korea on 16 August 1954. This Weasel is marked for the 58th vehicle in the line of march; note the white overspray around where the stencil for the A Company, 58th vehicle was placed on the bow. (National Archives)

Opposite below: Two members of a twelve-man cable-laying section of the 258th Signal Construction Company, 63rd Signal Battalion (OPR), help to lay a five-mile-long telephone line over the Hoch-Koenig Mountain between Ostpreussenhuette and Bluehmbach Castle in Austria on 18 January 1955. The phone line was being constructed to assist in future rescue operations in the mountains. The GIs are Cpl. Ray E. Paoli, left, and Pvt. F. Gv. Inderlin. (Nat onal Archives)

Appendix

GENERAL DATA

MODEL	T15
WEIGHT^	3400
LENGTH*	132
WIDTH*	60
HEIGHT*	67
TRACK*	42
STD TRACK WIDTH*	18
MAX SPEED LAND	32 MPH
MAX SPEED WATER	negligible
FUEL CAPY	
ELECTRICAL	12 negative
TRANSMISSION SPEEDS	3
TRANSFER CASE SPEEDS	2
TURNING RADIUS FEET	12

*Overall dimensions listed in inches.

ENGINE DATA

ENGINE MAKE/MODEL	Studebaker Champion
NUMBER OF CYLINDERS	6
CUBIC INCH DISPLACEMENT	170
HORSEPOWER	65 @ 3600
TORQUE	130 @ 1800
GOVERNED SPEED (rpm)	Not governed

T24 serial numbers and registration numbers

Quantity	Contract	Serial Numbers	Registration Numbers
1000	271-ORD-4023	3 through 1002	40121706 through 40122705
2	271-ORD-4235	1001 thru 1002	40136570 through 40136571
1000	271-ORD-4727	1003 thru 2002	40148307 through 40149306
100	271-ORD-4727	2003 thru 2102	40151152 through 40151251
1000	271-ORD-7197	2103 thru 3102	40151252 through 40152251

M29C serial numbers and registration numbers

Quantity	Contract	Serial Numbers	Registration Numbers
85	11-022-1515	3103 thru 3187	40176244 through 40176328
1000	11-022-1514	3188 thru 4187	40176329 through 40177328
60	11-022-1515	4188 thru 4247	40178110 through 40178169
1000	11-022-1519	4248 thru 5247	40178170 through 40179169
855	11-022-1515	5248 thru 6102	40179170 through 40180024
3400	11-022-2045	6103 thru 9502	40183801 through 40187200
1060	11-022-5369	9503 thru 10562	40193040 through 40194099
114	11-022-5904	10563 thru 10676	40194959 through 40195073

GENERAL DATA

MODEL	M29	M29C
WEIGHT (POUNDS)	3725	4778
LENGTH*	119	174
WIDTH*		
HEIGHT*	71	71
TRACK*	45	45
STD TRACK WIDTH*	20	20
MAX SPEED (MPH)	36	36
FUEL CAPACITY (US GALLONS)	35	35
RANGE (MILES)	175	175
ELECTRICAL (VOLTS)	12 negative ground	12 negative ground
TRANSMISSION SPEEDS	3	3
TRANSFER CASE SPEEDS	2	2
TURNING RADIUS (FEET)	12	12

*Overall dimensions listed in inches.

ENGINE DATA

ENGINE MAKE/MODEL	Studebaker Champion
NUMBER OF CYLINDERS	6
CUBIC INCH DISPLACEMENT	170
HORSEPOWER	65 @ 3600
TORQUE (POUND-FEET)	130 @ 1800
GOVERNED SPEED (rpm)	Not governed